MIRRORS OF THE MIND

METAPHORIC NARRATIVES IN HEALING

By

DR. NICOLE LEE　&　**DR. PETER MACK**
MBBS　　　　　　　MBBS, FRCS, PhD

Publication by *From the Heart Press*:
First Publication Feb 2015
Website: www.fromtheheartpress.com

Copyright: Peter Mack & Nicole Lee
ISBN: 978-0-9929248-5-0

All rights reserved. Except for brief quotations in critical articles or reviews, no part of this book may be reproduced in any manner without prior written permission from the publisher.

The rights of Dr. Peter Mack and Dr. Nicole Lee as authors have been asserted in accordance with the Copyright, Designs and Patents Act 1988.

A CIP catalogue record of this book is available from the British Library.

Book artist:
Ms. Wendy Mack
Email: wendy.mzf@gmail.com

Cover Design:
Ashleigh Hanson
Email: ash@shifted.co.nz

To contact the authors:
Dr. Nicole Lee
Email: nicole.leesq@gmail.com

Dr. Peter Mack
Email: dr.pmack@gmail.com
Website: http://www.petermack.sg

Disclaimer

The story and information provided in this book are designed to provide helpful information on regression hypnotherapy and to share the authors' experience in the process. The ideas and advice in this book are intended to promote a wider awareness of a therapeutic modality that has been underutilized. They are not intended as a substitute for consultation or treatment by a qualified mental health professional.

The names and identities of the people in the book have been disguised. The intention is to protect confidentiality while preserving the spirit of the work. No claim is made of any miraculous effectiveness of the therapy. Also, no therapists are advised to engage the powerful techniques of regression hypnotherapy in their practice unless they are adequately trained. The suitability of a patient for treatment must be assessed and individualized on the basis of his symptomatology, pathology, emotional makeup and belief system.

CONTENTS

Foreword		7
Introduction		9
Chapter 1:	Victim Mentality	21
	By: Dr. Nicole Lee	
Chapter 2:	Self-Empowerment	47
	By: Dr. Nicole Lee	
Chapter 3:	Guides, Soul and Higher Self	59
	By: Dr. Peter Mack	
Chapter 4:	The Path to Spirituality	65
	By: Dr. Nicole Lee	
Chapter 5:	Leap of Faith	71
	By: Dr. Nicole Lee	
Chapter 6:	Envy and Jealousy	81
	By: Dr. Nicole Lee	
Chapter 7:	Choice and Regret	95
	By: Dr. Nicole Lee	
Chapter 8:	Cosmic Reminders	105
	By: Dr. Nicole Lee	
Chapter 9:	Inner Healing	125
	By: Dr. Nicole Lee	
Chapter 10:	Tarot Imagery and Healing	139
	By: Dr. Peter Mack	
Chapter 11:	Paradox of the One and Many	155
	By: Dr. Nicole Lee	
Chapter 12:	A New Beginning	171
	By: Dr. Nicole Lee	
Chapter 13:	Purpose of Life	179
	By: Dr. Peter Mack	
Appendix I:	Imagination, Imagery and Healing	187
	By: Dr. Peter Mack	
Appendix II:	The Soul in Reincarnation	197
	By: Dr. Peter Mack	
Further Reading		203
Regression Therapy Associations		207

FOREWORD

This wonderful book is written by two medical doctors, and is about the healing journey of one of them. From a medical perspective healing is returning the physical body to the level of health it was at some earlier point. However, this book is about a holistic approach that accepts that the patient's problem is often a message about some aspect of life that is not working out. Holistic healing is about personal growth and becoming aware of the emotional cause of the problem and what needs to be done to change some aspect of thinking and the way of living. It offers personal growth through self-discovery and gives a deeper meaning of life.

Peter Mack, one of the authors, has been known to me for several years and I have published his earlier books on hypnosis and regression therapy. I can confirm his integrity and the highest professional standards he works to in his practice using therapy, just as he has for the last thirty years in the medical profession working as a surgeon in a Singapore hospital. Nicole Lee, the other author, has bravely stood up against the prevailing medical culture to share her healing journey with new ideas and thoughts. This includes how she learned to use the power of meditation and how regression therapy helped her to be able to tune into her own healing metaphors and stories, some perhaps past lives. It also includes how she allowed herself to be open to spiritual inspiration and her own inner wisdom.

Meditation has been proved to reduce people's stress, and has already started to be incorporated into the medical model. Metaphors are used in hypnosis, which has been widely accepted as a powerful healing tool by many countries – as early as 1955 by the British Medical Association, and in 1958 by the American Medical Association. Past life regression has been used in the West for over forty years and is becoming a more widespread tool to help in the healing process. For regression therapists it is not the truth of a past life story that is important, it's the way that it helps people find new answers to a current life problem and move forward.

If the reader has doubts about some of the approaches and procedures in the book, all they are asked to do is to have an open mind and know that the honesty and integrity of these doctors is intact. This is their story and their success. It is also a self-help inspiration to any reader who is prepared to try these ideas to have a more meaningful life.

Andy Tomlinson
January 2015

INTRODUCTION

"The turning point in the process of growing up is when you discover the core of strength within you that survives all hurt."

Max Lerner, 1959
In: The Unfinished Country

Part One – The Synchronicity
Dr. Nicole Lee

At the age of thirty-three I felt lost and painfully stuck in my life. For years, I had been trying to seek out the purpose behind my existence but to no avail. No matter how hard I tried or how many different paths I took, everything turned out to be in vain. I still ended up where I started, feeling unfulfilled and despondent. By now, I was tired and dispirited. I sensed myself losing the drive and motivation for change, and gradually lapsing into inactivity and complacency. Yet, underneath this confusing mix of emotions, I could not suppress my unhappiness and the mounting sense of urgency to search for my life purpose and identify who I truly am.

Out of the blue, something intriguing happened. My life started to turn around! I began to develop sudden insights into why things were happening the way they did. After all these years, it finally dawned on me that I had been searching for meaning in the wrong places! I had failed to see that the purpose of my life was essentially a *spiritual* quest. Negating my inner essence, I had been seeking for answers in the outer physical world. My focus on the physical world had completely overshadowed my spiritual awareness. I was hopelessly out of balance and lacked the awareness for inner discovery and growth.

As my life started to transform, an irresistible urge to share with others who might be facing the same difficulties surfaced. Instinctively, I engaged myself in writing this book to share my healing experience. Deep down, I knew my life would never be the same again.

I grew up in a typical Asian family with three younger siblings. Being the eldest had its perks as well as downsides. I was given my own bedroom while my three younger siblings had to cramp into one. However, being the eldest, I had to face up to the challenge of fulfilling high parental expectations.

From a young age, I had been under pressure to achieve good grades and top positions in school. As a perfectionist, I drove myself very hard. Since secondary school days, I planned my study schedules meticulously and months ahead, down to the hour. During school holidays, my daily schedule typically started at seven in the morning and ended around midnight. I spent ninety-five percent of my waking hours in studying. To cope with the situation, I curbed outings with friends and abstained from all entertainment, including television programs.

My solitude won me the reputation of "lacking a life" with my peers, and my fellow schoolmates branded me as an "exam slave". Yet, within me, I was aware that what actually drove me to this extreme lifestyle was not the urge for top grades, as everyone had thought, but rather, fear and guilt. It was the fear of under-achievement that might limit my future career options, which in turn would disappoint my parents. Then, there was the guilt feeling that every hour spent doing anything else other than studying was a waste of time. While it was a painful way to live, it was, unfortunately, the only way I knew.

Amid the hardships, I survived secondary and high school and was ready to go through the last league of my educational journey – university. Over the years I had developed a strong interest in Food Science and Technology, and was very keen to pursue the knowledge area at a tertiary level. However, after the release of my High School exam results, the "smothering parent syndrome" kicked in and I was told by my mother to study Medicine instead!

The reason given to me was that since there hadn't been any doctor in the family line, I ought to be the first to bring pride and glory to the family.

I was dejected. Becoming a doctor had never been my ambition. Nor had I ever envisaged that such a career would suit my pensive and introverted personality. Should I sacrifice my personal interest for the sake of obedience?

It was ironical. All this while, I had thought that by getting good grades, I would be able to choose my career option more freely for myself. Yet in the end, I was told to study Medicine because my grades were good enough! I struggled against the decision but soon relented in the face of mounting parental pressure. I failed to stand up for myself. My self-worth crumbled. The flicker of light disappeared, and my world fell into darkness.

Medical school was a torture. I continued my learner's role as an exam slave, and at a more intense pace. I had to study even harder because within the medical curriculum there were many more facts to be committed to memory. Life was a dread. I recalled freaking out a few times on the night before exams; I was so stressed that I thought I would snap. Many a time, I questioned the purpose of my life and wondered why I had to go through this torment. I constantly regretted my decision not to stand up for myself.

Miraculously, I survived the five years of undergraduate medical education. I graduated in 2005. I thought the ordeal was over, but little did I realize that a greater nightmare was awaiting me during the year of medical housemanship. Work life began very shortly after graduation, and went at a very fast pace. Within the hospital environment, I slogged hard, and stretched my limits of physical tolerance at times. It was not uncommon to work for a continuous stretch of thirty-six hours without sleep or rest, while running on one's feet, attending to patients' needs and performing medical procedures. In the absence of dedicated time for meals, Snickers bars had become my staple substitute for that year.

Ten months passed. I had become more accustomed to the work life and was looking forward to the end of the ordeal. Then to my horror, a needle-stick injury occurred. I pricked myself accidentally while performing a venepuncture procedure on a patient whose blood was subsequently tested positive for HIV antibodies. I went numb!

I was quickly started on anti-retrovirals (anti-HIV medication), suffered badly the side effects of the medication and experienced persistent nausea and giddiness for the next two weeks. Again I questioned myself: Why had I relented to my parents in the first place? Did I suffer all these years to end up contracting HIV? I prayed for this nightmare to end. Thankfully, when the HIV Western Blot (definitive test for HIV DNA) results came out a fortnight later, the patient was confirmed to be HIV negative. The earlier serology test was actually a false-positive. I had never felt more relieved.

I finally completed my housemanship year, and obtained full medical registration from the Medical Council. Henceforth, with a six-year bond to serve in the public healthcare sector, there was no question of my seeking employment elsewhere. I had no particular interest in any medical specialty then, and therefore did not proceed to apply for any traineeship position, unlike most of my classmates.

My first medical rotation as a Medical Officer was in Public Health. I felt relieved. It was an administrative post and the upside of that rotation was that it was a nine-to-five office-hour job. For the first time my life tempo slowed and I had some private time for myself.

After work, I began to enjoy some quiet moments during which I could do my leisure reading, self-reflection and soul-searching. I started reading books on self-help, motivation, self-improvement, religion and spirituality in the hope of finding meaning in my life. However, in the absence of a clear direction, I could not obtain clear answers. I also did not know how to apply the book concepts to my day-to-day life. For example, what could I do to "be more conscious" or to "live in the now"? How could I "connect with my spiritual self" when I could neither see nor touch it? And how could I be truly happy when there are so many unanswered questions?

While I knew everyone strives to be happy, the term "happiness" sounded like an ambiguous concept to me, or at best a foundational term that was not a means to anything else. Desiring happiness appears to be part of one's nature but few people seem to know how to acquire it. On my part, I did not feel any inner calling and was uncertain if I had a predestined life purpose. All that I had been doing hitherto appeared insignificant, non-purposeful and meaningless.

I recalled once asking a friend about his purpose of life, and what his personal understanding of the meaning of life was. After all, these were the same questions that I had been constantly asking myself. His response shocked me! I remembered his chuckle, and as he gently patted me on my shoulder, he said, "You think too much!" Till this day I can still vividly see his quizzical look.

I was baffled. How could the search for one's purpose and meaning in life be an act of rumination or over-contemplation? Wouldn't the answer be the foundation for what we should be doing in life? However, I eventually realized that this was a very typical and consistent reaction from most, if not all, of my friends and family members, whenever the same question was posed.

Frustration continued to build up. At the age of twenty-five, I did not know what I wanted for myself. I had hoped for a career that I could enjoy, but it did not happen. I could not force myself to like Medicine as a career, but I had a bond to serve. Why had I imposed years of studying and hardship upon myself only to face more uncertainty and doubt?

I felt trapped. I was desperate for a vision to hold on to while serving my bond. I also needed a reason to make my years of struggle appear worthwhile. As time passed, the feeling of unease and urgency escalated, but no answers emerged. All I could do was to continue to read more fervently. At one point, I came across the book *Messages from the Masters* by Dr. Brian Weiss, and became intrigued with the phenomenon of hypnosis.

Dr. Weiss is a renowned psychiatrist in the United States and a medical pioneer in past life regression. In the course of his practice, he encountered a unique patient who, under hypnosis, spontaneously regressed back to a past life. Since then he has recognized the healing value of past life regression and has been actively promoting it as a means to establishing wellbeing. I found the past life stories in his book amazing, and began to wonder if hypnotherapy could be a vehicle for me to search for my life purpose.

My job posting in Public Health was also where I first met Dr. Mack for the first time. He was seconded from a public hospital to work as a part-time advisor to the Ministry of Health on policy matters. He would come to the Ministry's office thrice a week and work in the cubicle next to mine, but he kept to himself most of the time. Given our age gap, we hardly talked, but as time passed, we warmed to each other and became friends. Little did I realize that he would eventually become a major source of influence in my life.

The years passed. I rotated through various medical disciplines in the course of my employment but had not developed interest in any particular specialty. Work got much busier after leaving Public Health. Neither reading nor self-reflection had brought me any nearer to the answers I was searching for. I started to despair, and my quest came to a halt. Life became a drag. I literally existed from day to day and felt I was not truly living.

I subsequently left hospital practice and moved on to the private sector to work as a general practitioner. This was also the time when I got married to a fellow doctor who had been giving me moral support. I practiced Family Medicine responsibly but it was not a career that I was passionate about. I remained unhappy and gradually began to look for career options outside Medicine.

I picked up an interest in Finance and subsequently pursued a part-time Master degree course. Perhaps the added qualification would open a new career or life path, I thought. I later realized that this was too simplistic a view, and I was soon guided by common sense to abandon the move. I was disappointed once again.

With this setback, I became increasingly insecure. The angst, frustration, and dissatisfaction with my work life were overwhelming. I felt despondent in looking for the "right" job that would allow me to start living more meaningfully. I felt I was simply wasting my prime by being stuck in a place that I did not want to be in; yet I could not see a breakthrough. Hopelessness was sinking in, and nothing seemed worth struggling for.

This was the time when an unexpected email from Dr. Mack literally turned my life around. We had not contacted each other for five years. In fact I had once thought of initiating contact, but I felt somewhat ashamed to let him know that I was still stuck at where we last left off. When he asked me how I had been, I was truly surprised and elated! I responded immediately and we met over lunch to catch up on each other's progress. What was intended to be a casual meeting eventually turned out to be a pivotal event in my life.

I recalled the last time we had lunch together was seven years ago. I was still working in the public sector then, and had arranged to return him a book that I had earlier borrowed from him. I could remember how I confided in him my frustrations and work challenges. This time round, it struck me that his capacity for empathic listening had not changed. I felt touched and could not resist sharing with him the limbo state that I had gotten myself into.

One might have called this an act of meaningful coincidence or synchronicity. When I realized that he had been using regression hypnotherapy to help his patients over and above his clinical work in Surgery, I could not stop myself from asking him for help. It turned out that this was the start of a series of life-changing experiences, leading on to my long-awaited path of personal transformation.

"Life is not about negative circumstances that happen to you, it's about what you do with the golden opportunities hidden within!"

Rhonda Byrne
In: Hero

Part Two – The Challenge
Dr. Peter Mack

At the point when I reconnected with Nicole, I realized that she had remained unhappy since we last met. There was sadness in her gaze and the low-spirited tonality of her voice gave away the clue that things were not well. She believed that she had not been living a life that made sense, nor was she convinced that what she had achieved in her career so far was something fruitful. She gave me the sense that she had been crying out for meaning and was in need of help. Beneath her issues was an emotional turmoil that she had difficulty grappling with.

A loss of meaning is central to one's suffering and unhappiness, but it is the emotion pervading all the sensory experiences that gives those sensations their meaning. In Nicole's case, her reaction to her mother's approach in handling her tertiary education was one of shock and disbelief. This had effectively interrupted all meaningful thought on her part.

Emotions are generally an important organizer of meaning and provider of directions for one's thoughts and behavior. When Nicole failed to make sense of her world she responded to her suffering by searching for a meaning that could make sense of her perceived misfortune.

I soon realized that it was a sense of victimization that had contradicted her fundamental belief about herself. The world therefore no longer seemed a fair place for her to live in. She questioned whether she was a good enough person to deserve a decent life. This meaning vacuum was taking her a long time to repair. The earlier life event had defined her as the "loser" and she now had to find a new assumption about her identity, work and career that made sense. Her qualities of trust and confidence needed to be recovered.

Nicole's request for therapy had come as a surprise. Helping others to find life purpose is not something that is talked about in medical school, let alone taught as a therapeutic skill. Her problem was vague and ambiguous and a seedbed for a whole set of other related questions: Why am I here? Why am I unhappy? Is there a higher goal that I am supposed to achieve in my life? How am I supposed to help myself? Will the meaning of life, once discovered, unlock all the other mysteries of life?

Unfortunately, Nicole's concept of life purpose was closely knitted with that of a career, and that made things more difficult. Her perceived obstacle to finding a solution to her life issue rested with the uncertainty as to how she could transit from her current job into a more "purposeful" one. She could not see the uniqueness in her individual self. She found herself moving through molasses and at a snail's pace for no apparent reason. Although she had been looking out for things that she felt might make her happy, there were repeated let-downs and disappointments.

Understanding Nicole's definition of success was a challenge. Was it about a comfortable life? A satisfying job? The amount of money she earned? Or was it simply acquiring those things that make her feel good? There was no clarity at that point.

This book is essentially a chronicle of Nicole's healing journey, and it reveals the way in which life stressors can be transformed into learning experiences. It involves the wisdom of Nicole surrendering herself to the journey instead of forcing things to go her way. From this journey, she had understood that much of what she thought she wanted for her life had come from her ego-self.

The ego can be understood as that part of us that cares only for our own happiness. It is, in other words, the spoiled, petulant child within each of us. It cares only for our own comfort and our own gain. When an individual sets goals and objectives from this state of mind, he is often disappointed, because these goals serve only his immediate whims and desires.

There is an inner wisdom in each of us. When Nicole set her ego aside and allowed her inner self to assume control, things became clearer. Not only was she able to choose more lasting and satisfying goals, she also became clearer about a more efficient way of achieving them. With time, she understood how fear and struggle could be transformed into positive qualities such as confidence and trust. Putting personal preferences aside had not been easy. She was stuck for a long time with doing things in a certain way, and was expecting a specific outcome from her efforts. It took her time and patience to gain greater awareness of those instances where she has been clinging on to situations and pushing circumstances.

Gradually Nicole learned how to keep her expectations in check. She shifted her focus from defining her life purpose with a statement to identifying the broad themes of her personal mission. As she learned to grow and develop, so did her life purpose.

The approach to healing had taken several forms. For the greater part, I had chosen the self-disclosure approach. This provided room for Nicole to talk about her emotional reactions to her painful life events, and was carried out under trance. It allowed her bottled-up tension to be released within a controlled environment. The reopening of communication between her emotions and the processes of cognitive adaption allowed her to understand her past better and regain beliefs of fairness challenged by earlier life experiences. Tough lessons and difficult-to-interpret messages were at the heart of every regression session that we went through. "That everything is a choice" was one such example that emerged. With the healing that accompanied the process, she has since brought to light her inner strength – the power to be herself and to live the life she wants.

The quality of the mental imagery that was elicited in this healing journey was a surprise for both of us. The blend of symbols, metaphors and narratives provided a fertile ground for establishing communication with her dialogical self. As answers to her existential questions emanated, she found the metaphoric "mirrors" were the vehicle for change and transformational growth.

It was Nicole's choice to use an autobiographical mode for her narratives in this book. This provided room for her to freely express her personal feelings of her healing experience. I have added explanatory notes in shaded boxes wherever appropriate, and interspersed them with the story text so as to minimize distraction from the story flow.

A special chapter on Tarot-based healing has been included. While at first sight the chapters may appear to be somewhat out of place, the intent was to illustrate how an appreciation of the Tarot symbolism that appeared in Nicole's meditation had a way of attaching meaning to her life issues. In addition, the theoretic aspects of imagination and mental imagery have been included in the appendix to address Nicole's initial doubts on creative visualization.

This book is targeted at readers from the general public, but it is hoped to be also a significant step forward in convincing our medical colleagues of the healing power of the mind-body-soul connection.

CHAPTER ONE

Victim Mentality

Dr. Nicole Lee

"There is a fine line between compassion and a victim mentality. Compassion though is a healing force and comes from a place of kindness towards yourself. Playing the victim is a toxic waste of time that not only repels other people, but also robs the victim of ever knowing true happiness."

Bronnie Ware, 2012
In: The Top Five Regrets of the Dying

Meditation was something which I had never seriously practiced. I recalled my first attempt at meditation some years back and remembered that the experience amounted to nothing beyond a few minutes of increased thought activity. I came to the conclusion that I had a "monkey" mind and its hyperactive state hindered any efforts to persist further. This time, I was taken by surprise that Dr. Mack had insisted that I was to commit myself to regular daily meditative exercises. The reason he gave was that such exercises would optimize my mental state to reap the full benefits of regression therapy. At the same time, he also encouraged me to start a journal to document my thoughts, reflections and emotions. Given my penchant for writing, I gladly acted on it.

In the interim, I read Dr. Mack's book, *Healing Deep Hurt Within,* and that gave me a fair idea of what to expect during hypnotherapy. His second book, *Life-Changing Moments in Inner Healing*, opened my mind further as to how the retrieval of past life memories could be a powerful tool for healing.

Shortly after our meeting, I began my meditative exercises regularly and seriously. Initially, whenever I closed my eyes, thoughts and worries on recent problems crowded in. It was distracting. After several attempts, I took a slightly different approach and concentrated on my breaths instead. I started to focus on my inhalation and exhalations, followed them all the way through and quickly became mindful of them. My mental discourse stopped and I had, in the process, brought my mind home. I did not think of my worries anymore. Nor did I have to make a conscious effort to stop generating unwanted thoughts.

Next, something unexpected happened.

While I was focusing on my breath and learning to enjoy it, a unique imagery emerged. For the first time my mental stillness was sustained. Suddenly a mental picture of a grassland appeared and I saw myself galloping on a horse across it. It was a pleasant surprise.

Initially, I could not understand nor appreciate the significance of this imagery and was under the impression that my thoughts had gone astray. I consciously suppressed the image, and restarted the process. This happened several times, but to my surprise, the same image reappeared consistently at every attempt. I eventually accepted and worked with it. Little did I know that this was the starting point of a series of amazing stories that flooded my subsequent therapy sessions.

I noticed I had "tamed" my mind rather quickly and I was delighted with my progress. With practice, my visualization ability steadily improved. I could focus my mind for increasingly longer durations at each meditative sitting. At the same time, I noticed that my intuitive ability had sharpened. Soon, I found myself able to connect with my Higher Self in the meditative state, after some guidance from Dr. Mack.

A fortnight later I felt I was ready to undergo my first therapy session.

Session 1 (Regression): The Princess who left the English Castle for the Red Cottage

It was the afternoon of 20 May 2014 when I stepped into Dr. Mack's clinic. He had set aside special time for me. After his initial round of explanations to demystify the phenomenon of hypnosis, I was still a little apprehensive. I was anxious if I could successfully visualize the imagery needed for healing.

My hands felt clammy and I wiped them on my pants while no one was watching. As the clock ticked, I reminded myself to suspend my judgment and trust my instincts. In the meantime I relaxed on the reclining couch. The air-conditioned room was cold and a nurse came over to give me a blanket to keep warm for the session.

I closed my eyes. Next I heard music being turned on and soon the room was primed with soothing sounds with base tones of a healing frequency. As the music flowed, I relaxed more readily. It was as if the musical vibrations were interacting and harmonizing with my emotional self. The low tones, the deep basses and the drums had an earthly feel with a strong emotional upwelling. An occasional higher musical note would inject some sense of flightiness as the vibration became a little faster.

A minute later, I heard some verbal instructions being delivered in a low-toned voice. I realized the induction phase of the therapy was about to begin.

"Keep your eyes closed and take a deep breath." I recognized it as Dr. Mack's voice.

"As you breathe in slowly, focus on the air entering your chest until you reach a peak, and when you breathe out, focus on the air leaving your chest. Remember, as you inhale, you breathe in relaxation to your body, and when you exhale, you breathe out the tension from your body."

After three slow, deep breaths, I felt distinctly more relaxed. At the next set of instructions, I recognized that the script was one of progressive muscular relaxation.[1] I was asked to relax various muscle groups of the body in turn, starting with the scalp and face, followed by the neck, chest and abdomen, and ending with the thighs and legs. By the time the relaxation reached the feet and toes, I had drifted into a dreamy state.

Next, I was asked to lift my eyelids and open my eyes, but to my intrigue, they felt so heavy that I did not even want to lift them. I later learned that this was part of the eyelid-catalepsy test[2] that was meant as a check for trance depth.

Next, I felt my trance deepening as I was guided to imagine a staircase down which I was descending, and with every step that I took down the stairs, I went deeper and deeper into the hypnotic state. I could visualize a spiral staircase leading downwards, and saw myself descending step by step as numbers were being counted. Soon, I found myself already at the bottom of the stairs, ahead of Dr. Mack's instructions. Not knowing what to do next, I hesitated and consciously paused my imagery while waiting for his count to complete.

Next, the scene of a comfortable bed was described to me. I was guided to rest on it. I could feel the coziness of the soft mattress as I saw myself lying on it. As Dr. Mack suggested raindrops falling from the sky and streaking down the window panes, I could vividly see the image of the water droplets and hear the sound of the rain hitting the glass. As I continued with the guided imagery, I was then led out of the bedroom into a "healing garden". At this point a mystical scene took over.

"You see a mist building up in front of you, and instinctively you are attracted to walk towards it. In a moment, as you are getting closer to the mist, I will be counting from one to three.

---

[1] Progressive muscle relaxation is a technique first described by Dr. Edmund Jacobsen in the early 1920's for controlling the state of muscle tension. It has since been used by hypnotists worldwide as an induction script to guide a patient into trance.

[2] Muscle catalepsy is one of several strange phenomena that is produced while a subject is under hypnosis, and is related to trance depth.

One ... you take your first step and walk into the mist, and two ... you find yourself walking right into the middle of the mist."

As these words were being spoken, I saw a dense white mist enveloping me, obscuring all views. I could feel my heart beating slightly faster, as I felt the anticipation of what might appear when I walked out of the mist.

"At the next step, three ... you are walking out of the mist into a time of the past."

Suddenly, at hearing those words, I sensed a blinding light. Gradually, as my eyes adjusted to the brightness, the first image that I saw on coming out of the mist was an endless stretch of grass plains!

For a moment I was stunned. It was the very same image that I had been repeatedly visualizing and suppressing during my earlier meditation attempts! This time, the same image reappeared under hypnotic guidance. I was terribly excited, and chose to let it emerge freely.

Next I heard another instruction: "As the mist is clearing, tell me where you are and what is happening." Instinctively I knew it was time for me to speak up, even though I was under trance.

"I see an endless stretch of grass plains," I began. "The sky is blue and the air is fresh. I am a young girl about seven to eight years of age. I am dressed in peasant's clothing, and my hair is tied in two braids down my shoulders."

"What are you doing on the grass plains?" I was asked.

"I look around and I am happy being there. I like the grass plains and the sense of freedom. I love the space, the wind, and the smell of fresh grass tickling my senses. I feel blissful."

"Is there anybody next to you?"

This question induced me to look around, and I sensed that I could not see any other people.

"No one ..." I replied, and paused.

By now I was completely embodied into the regression scene and was beginning to appreciate the concept of the "hidden observer".³ What this means is that there are two levels of awareness operating within myself at the same time. A part of me was experiencing myself as a young girl on a dream-like journey, while another part of me was dissociated from what was going on in the story, and continued to exercise objectivity in observing the hypnotic process.⁴

> **Therapist's Note (1): On Mental Imagery**
> **Dr. Peter Mack**

Nicole was easily hypnotizable and the fact that her mental imagery went ahead of my hypnotic script was an indication that her imaginative process was innately rich.

Guided imagery is often utilized in regression because it is an efficient way of assisting memory recall and facilitating entry into an imaginal scene. The concept of mental imagery was described as far back in 1883 by Francis Galton. When first applied to psychotherapy in the early twentieth century, it appeared in the form of predetermined scenes as points for departure. In this session the starting point for therapy session was made up of a spontaneous image that Nicole had allowed to appear on her mind screen. It was the picture of a grassland, and it opened up her mind to a metaphoric story.

After some moments I continued.

"I see a barn now. There is a lot of hay stacked on the ground. I see a brown horse tethered by a pole on the left side of the barn. I walk up to the horse and pet it on its nose lovingly. He is my horse."

---

[3] The "hidden observer" is a form of hypnotic dissociation described by Hilgard in 1977 in *The Divided Consciousness*. This is exemplified in regression therapy when the patient imagines herself returning to an earlier age while another part of her mind remains in the present.

[4] The two levels of awareness are powered differently in terms of neurophysiology. The theta brain waves (4–8Hz) are responsible for generating the dream-like images while the beta waves (12–30Hz) maintain a background level of awareness to allow the patient to evaluate the dream-like experience in a more rational manner.

"What happens next?"

"I am alone and I am just waiting."

"Do you have a sense of whom you are waiting for?"

There was something special about the probing nature of the question, the manner in which I was asked and the appropriateness of the moment it was posed. Upon hearing the question, a sudden surge of fear and loneliness arose from deep within me. I could not suppress it. The wave of emotion gathered momentum and rapidly swept right through me. I started to cry uncontrollably, surprising even myself.

Therapist's Note (2): On Catharsis
Dr. Peter Mack

While emotion is a natural body reaction and a way of dealing with hurtful experiences, crying is often a biological necessity for healing to take place. Unfortunately, as adults, most of us have unlearned this ability as part of the socialization process. As a result, many of us have accumulated large amounts of repressed emotion and body tension which are not recognized. This interferes with our thought and perception processes.

The concept of catharsis has been brought into the field of psychotherapy by Sigmund Freud. In regression therapy, regular use is made of catharsis for its healing property. By re-enacting scenes from her past (including past lives) the patient brings unconscious conflicts into her consciousness.

Catharsis manifests as an explosive release of deeply troubled, deeply rooted states of suffering within the individual. The catharsis evoked in Nicole revealed the long-standing emotions that had been buried but were now allowed to be discharged. With the release of the deeply held energy there was momentary access to the wound that was underlying her life issue. This created an opportunity to become aware of what the wound was about.

I would have expected that anyone crying the way I did would have made the observer feel uncomfortable and awkward. Paradoxically, I heard an opposite response in the background.

"Let it out ... It's okay to let it out. Let it out all the way!" I was surprised that I was being encouraged to release my emotions.

I followed the suggestion and let my tears flow. There was some relief as the tension was relieved. I was still crying as I continued to describe what I was experiencing. "I am now squatting on the floor, hugging myself and crying uncontrollably. I am waiting for my family. I do not know where they are."

"What has happened?"

"It is only the grassland, the horse and me now. I do not know what to do. I am sad and lonely. I hope to see someone else but there is no one around. I am all alone and helpless, with no one to depend on." I continued to sob.

"What has happened to your family?"

An image of a fire burning the house came to my mind, and instinctively I knew what happened. "There was a fire," I said. "Everyone in the house died. I was playing on the grassland and escaped. When I went back to the house, everything is gone. Only the barn is left. I don't know where my family members are. I don't see them around."

"How did the fire happen?"

"Someone set the house on fire. It is somebody who hates the family but I do not know who he is. Now I just see myself pulling the horse out of the barn. I get on it and ride away. I am crying as I ride the horse across the grassland. Suddenly, I see someone on a black horse is chasing me from behind! I keep looking over my shoulders. I don't know who he is and I am very scared."

"What happens next?"

"I ride harder, and see an iron gate ahead leading into a town. I ride through the gate, and get off the horse. I now see the black horse behind me stopping outside the gates. There is a man riding on it but I cannot see who he is. He just turns his horse around and leaves."

I had absolutely no idea of the significance of the man on the black horse at this stage. However, as the therapy evolved over the next few weeks, I subsequently uncovered his identity as part

of a most fascinating story when the pieces of the puzzle fell into place. (Session 15)
"What did you do next?"
"I feel relieved, and start to survey my surroundings. I get down the horse and walk through the streets. The houses are made of mud. But I do not see anybody. There is no sign of life."
"Which country and era might this be?"
"It appears to be the sixteenth or seventeenth century, in a small English town."
"As you are walking through the town, tell me what your thoughts are."
"I am wondering what is going on and where everyone is. I am also curious why this man on the black horse did not follow me into the town. I feel very tired. I reach the end of the street. There is a shiny, white castle that contrasts starkly with the dirty, mud town. How strange! I am outside, looking at the castle. I don't know if I should go in. So in the end, I pull the horse into one of the mud houses outside the castle and just wait. I dare not go in. It is already dark. So I just wait in the mud house together with the horse. Soon I fall asleep."
"Go to the point where you wake up from your sleep and describe to me what happens?"
"I walk out of the mud house to look at the castle again. I am still afraid to enter it."
Next, I was guided to enter the castle. I took a deep breath and focused my mind as I visualized myself walking past the castle gate. A blurry image of the interior of the castle emerged, but I could still make out certain features. The feeling was a strange one.
"The castle looks empty," I exclaimed. "The ceiling is high and pointed. I cannot see the details very well. I see a throne in the middle of the hall. It is gold in color. Everything inside appears new. There is nobody within. I walk up to the throne and touch the right arm rest. It feels smooth and cool."
At this point my imagery came to a halt and the story did not progress. I was then prompted to move to the next event.

Gradually, another image of myself at a different age emerged. I suddenly feel excited again at the development.

"I am now a princess in the castle. I am much older now, about seventeen or eighteen years of age. I am wearing a beautiful long, flowing white dress. I am sitting by a fountain in a beautiful garden. There are sculptures, elaborate fountains and beautiful flowers. I look at my reflection in the water, and I look fair and beautiful. I see a few lady servants in the garden, but all their heads are bowed."

"What are your emotions now?"

"Despite all the riches I now have, I sense that I am not happy. It is as if I am trapped in the castle forever. I yearn for the freedom of the grass plains. I am waiting to get out of the castle. Although I live in comfort and should be grateful for what I have, I am still not happy."

"What are you looking for to make yourself happier?"

"I want to go out, ride a horse in the grassland and be free again."

"What is stopping you?"

"If I leave, I will lose everything. I am trapped in my own dilemma."

A feeling of tiredness was overcoming me at this stage and my mind started to drift. Somehow Dr. Mack sensed my restlessness, deepened my trance state.

"I have decided to leave," I continued. "I am now standing in front of the iron gate of the town. I hold the reins of my brown horse in my left hand, and look back at the white castle one more time. I have nothing on my back. I push open the gates, get onto the horse and ride across the plains. I feel alive again. The wind blows across my face ... I do not know where to go but at least I am not trapped anymore. I go back to see the ruins of the burned house and the barn. Everything is old and dusty now. There is still nobody around."

"What are your feelings now as you are looking at the barn?"

"Very sad and lonely, but I know I am older now. It is time to leave the past behind and move on."

"Is there a lesson that you can learn from this?"

"I am not sure. I just sense her feeling of loneliness now ... She is very lost, so am I in my present life." Unconsciously I had somehow dissociated myself from the image and started to use the third person instead of the first person, in my dialogue.

"What is it that she's looking for, that you think will make her happy?"

"She wants her home again. She wants her own place where she can go to, and where she can be happy and where she is not trapped anymore. Now she does not know where to go."

"Is there a parallel that you can see with your present life?"

"I think I am just like her now, standing in the middle of nowhere, looking at the past, but just no idea where I am going next."

Next, I was guided to another significant event of this same life.

"I see a river, and I am still holding on to the horse. I follow the river downstream. It is the same horse I had when I was seven years of age. I am very grateful that he is still with me. The river now leads into a forest, and I know I have to get through the forest. I keep walking, until I finally see some light at the end of the forest, it's very bright."

"Where does the light come from?"

"It is another stretch of open plains but there is a red cottage a short distance away from the end of the forest. I see smoke coming out of the chimney. It looks very warm and inviting. I bring the horse and walk towards it. There is a plump lady dressed in peasant's clothing standing in front of the house, carrying a basket of bread. She has a very friendly and smiling face."

"What happens next?"

"She sees that my clothes are dirty and concludes that I must have traveled a long way. 'Come into the house and I will keep you warm,' she says. I am grateful for her invitation. She is an English lady with round rosy cheeks. She opens the door and I step in."

I then focused my mind to visualize the interior of the cottage.

"The first thing I see is the warm fireplace. The cottage is very cozy. I see a young boy, about five to six years old. He is playing with some wooden toys. He looks up curiously at me when I walk in. The lady tells me to keep warm while she prepares some food. Outside, I hear a man leading my horse into the stables. I sit at a wooden table by the fire. The boy puts down his toy and comes up to me. He places his hand on my left knee, but he does not speak. The lady brings me a bowl of warm soup. She bends over and places it in front of me. I look up at her smiling face."

"Focus on this lady and see if she is someone whom you know in your present life."

Upon hearing this instruction, I suddenly see the image of my mother's face superimposed onto the English lady's face!

"Oh ... she is my mother!" I blurted out.

Once again, the urge to cry was overwhelming and I could not control the tears streaming down my face. I went into catharsis once more.

"How do you feel now that you know she is your mother?"

"I cannot believe it ... This lady is so warm and kind to me, whereas my mother in my present life is anything but warm and kind!" (crying)

After a while, as my emotions subsided, I saw someone entering the cottage.

"A man walks into the house. He is tall and strong. He looks younger than the lady. I am not sure how he is related to the lady. He is the one who led my horse to the stable. He is dressed like a farmer or a peasant. I am trying to figure out if the boy is the son of the lady or the man ... but it feels like he is the child of neither of them. How weird! All of us just sit down at the wooden table and eat. They have not asked me anything. Soon I feel tired. I am falling asleep by the fireplace."

At this stage, Dr. Mack decided to bring the session to an end. I felt very tired as the session ended but the whole sequence of imagery fascinated me tremendously because of its level of visual reality. I could not help but ask: "How do I know that I have not imagined all that I visualized? And I wasn't hallucinating, right?"

Each image in the story had popped up spontaneously by itself, and I knew for sure that I did not actively plot the sequence of the story. If I did not imagine the story, where did the content come from? And how would I know if the event "really" happened? But again, it did not seem to be a true historical event, nor likely a past life event, given the setting of an empty town and grand castle in the middle of nowhere.

Therapist's Note (3): On Imagination
Dr. Peter Mack

Working with mental imagery and allowing it to unfold into scenes is a hypnotic process and it requires a certain trust in the power of creative imagination. Very often, however, the word "imagination" is used as a put-down on a regression story by non-believers of hypnosis. It implies that all the story content has been falsified. Attributing the story and imagery to imagination begs a bigger question: "Just what is imagination?" We all know what it is like to imagine, but that alone does not explain where the images come from, nor how they are produced.

The unlimited potential of the mind to create, transform and heal is only just beginning to be understood. More of the theoretical aspects will be given in Appendix I. Suffice to say, at this point, that if we are to be open to the vast power of imagination, we need a branch of psychology knowledge that honors not only the human mind, but also the soul and spirit.

We tried to make some meaning out of the regression story, but realized that there were insufficient clues at that stage. We both felt that the story was more metaphorical than historical. Whatever it was, there was no way of verifying if it was truly a past life event. At the end of the day, it would not matter, as long as the story conveyed a special meaning for me, and helped me to figure out the direction in life I wanted to go. Dr. Mack promised me that he would address this issue of imagination at a later session. I nodded with gratefulness. Little did we realize that we would eventually revisit this story at a later date, and under most intriguing circumstances. (Chapter 11)

As I headed home that evening, I felt extremely tired. It was as if I was suffering from a severe jet lag. My head was heavy. I headed to bed early that night, still wondering about the significance of the content of my first hypnotherapy experience. I did not expect that the answer would surface spontaneously during the quiet moment of my privacy two days later.

Session 2 (Regression): Sadness and the Early Years

"The cure for pain is in the pain." – Rumi

I turned up at the clinic again the next day. After a good night's rest, I was eager for a follow-up session. The puzzle of the regression story yesterday was still hovering in my mind but I decided not to let that interfere with the ongoing therapy.

Back on the reclining couch, I made myself comfortable and was able to relax and participate with much greater confidence this time. After three deep breaths, I was guided to visualize a "safe place" that I wished to belong to and in which I could feel secure and comfortable.

An image of a forest gradually emerged. Somehow I felt relaxed and happy at the sight of the green, natural environment. The silence of the still forest had a calming effect. The air was rich with earthly smells and a chirp from a nearby bird lured me into fascination. I knew it was time to start talking.

Therapist's Note (4): The "Safe Place"
Dr. Peter Mack

In general, patients who have experienced previous hurt will need to establish a safe place in which they can make sense of their experience and gain supremacy over them during psychotherapy.

For traumatized individuals, the issue of concern is always whether he will be hurt once again during the therapy session, or whether he will be free from further hurt.

The safe place being developed here is the psychic space between Nicole and myself, contained by the therapeutic relationship between us. As hypnosis is the vehicle for therapy, mental imagery could be conveniently used to create a place that is visually pleasant and psychologically secure. This place turned out to be a forest that she would revisit repeatedly in her subsequent therapy sessions. Also, this forest seemed to be evolving into a "healing metaphor" as her therapy progressed.

"I am in a forest, lying on the grass. There is a stream just in front of me. Water is flowing. There are fishes in the stream. I am surrounded by trees and the sunlight is streaming through the leaves of trees. I can feel the warmth of the sunlight and the coolness of the stream at the same time. It feels wonderful. I see rabbits and other living things."

"Focus on the rabbits and allow a feeling to emerge."

"These animals are just warm and innocent."

"Concentrate on the warmth and the innocence of the animals, and as you do so, allow a thought to emerge."

"I see myself cradling my pet chick that was given to me when I was in primary school. I like caressing its smooth feathers and feeling its warm body. I feel sad because the chick passed away shortly after, and it was my first pet."

"Go back to the last time you experienced this same feeling of sadness."

Again, my tears started to flow involuntarily. I felt an immense sadness engulfing me.

"My whole life is sad," I said.

Before I knew what happened, this emotion-laden statement quickly connected me to an event that took place fourteen years ago. I saw my sad self in the premises of the Administrative Building of the National University of Singapore (NUS). I had just finished Junior College then and had wanted to study Food

Science and Technology very much, but then I was being offered a place in the Faculty of Medicine instead.

Next moment I went into catharsis and was crying bitterly!

"I am at NUS, holding on to the phone, standing by the hallway and speaking to my mother. She tells me to choose Medicine over Food Science and Technology." I started to cry again, because that was not what I wanted. "My mother asks me to call a neighbor who is a law student and whom my mother feels will speak some 'sense' into me ..."

"What are your emotions now?"

"I am really confused and upset because I really do not want to study Medicine, but I also do not want to disobey my mother. The law-student neighbor tells me to choose Medicine too. So I feel very helpless!"

"Did you tell the law student about your feelings?"

"No. She is just trying to help, so I do not blame her."

"So what happens next?"

"I walk over to the Administration Office of the Faculty of Medicine and tell the person in charge that I will take up the offer to study Medicine."

"How do you feel after you have done that?"

"Very heavy-hearted. I feel I am reliving that scene right now ... I feel lost and hopeless. I wonder if my life would have been significantly different if I had picked a different choice."

"Did you let your mother know how you felt?"

"No, I didn't." I sighed. "Actually, over the years when she saw how unhappy I was, she realized it."

"Do you feel like letting her know now?"

I heard the question, but I hesitated in responding. In fact, deep down in my heart, I kind of understood why my mum had behaved in that manner. Not having had the opportunity of a higher education herself, she started working at a young age, but had to stop because she had to take care of the children. Admittedly she had sacrificed a lot for the family. As my siblings and I were growing up, she expressed her keen desire to have a doctor in the family as that would bring pride to everyone.

While all these thoughts and events were flashing through my mind, I suddenly noticed a turn in the style and approach of the therapy process. Instead of being posed with another question, I was suddenly asked to carry out a command.

"Now I want you to visualize your mother in front of you," I was clearly told.

This was a powerful suggestion. The image of my mother suddenly appeared in my mind's eye. I saw her standing in front of me. Over the next ten minutes of the therapy, I was directed to talk to my mother, and encouraged to express my innermost feelings and say what I had always wanted to say to her but never had a chance.

With this, I sank myself into a sea of indignation and sorrow. While remaining in trance, I revealed to my mother angrily how much she had hurt me with what she did. I told her in no uncertain terms how unhappy I had since become.

The momentum continued and I went into a full-blown catharsis. I cried bitterly. As I continued to vent out my frustrations and helplessness, I suddenly and unexpectedly saw my mother crying in remorse in response to my unhappiness!

I gave another deep sigh. After ten minutes of dialogue with my mother, interspersed with cathartic release, I slowly regained my composure and continued.

"She says she only did what she knew. I just want to forgive her and move on. It is so tiring," I said. "I also wish that I was stronger at that point in time, and had stood up for what I wanted. I wish that I'd had the courage to say 'no' and choose my own path. In fact I have been blaming myself all these years too, for my weakness and passivity."

"So are you still angry with her now?"

I hesitated, not knowing what to say.

After a long pause, I gathered enough courage and responded, "I think she is just as lost as any of us. I do not want to be angry with her anymore ... I have forgiven her."

A sense of relief seemed to have pervaded my whole body as I affirmed my willingness to forgive. It was a choice that I made, and the resulting change in feeling was indescribable.

"Now that you have decided to forgive her, I want you to see yourself walking over to give her a hug. Tell her you still love her and are ready to forgive her but she must appreciate that she does not impose her wishes on you again in future."

I sensed a pillow was being handed over to me at this point. I readily held on to it against my chest and hugged it as if my mother was in my arms. The sense of forgiveness was alive and flowing in and through me. There was a sudden shift in my thinking towards my mother accompanied by a sudden decision to let go of the ill-will. This was immediately followed by a natural resolution of grief on my part.

"Did she say anything to you?" Dr. Mack asked.

"Her tears are over her face. She says she has always loved me. It is just that she thinks I do not know what I want for myself." As I said these words, I realized that I had to let go of all these years of blame before I could move on in my current life. I subsequently learned from Dr. Mack that what I had just gone through was part of a psychodrama process.

Therapist's Note (5): On Psychodrama
Dr. Peter Mack

Psychodrama is an action method of therapy in which the patient is allowed to use role playing, self-presentation and spontaneous dramatization to gain insights into his interpersonal relationship with another individual. This method was developed by Jacob Moreno (1889–1974) and had features of theatre acts.

There are three dimensions in a psychodrama experience. Firstly it is dreamy in nature and more so when performed under trance. Secondly, it feels as if the re-enacted event is happening at the very moment of the role-playing. Thirdly, it is a memory that has come alive again after being evoked. As such, Nicole was able to reflect on it and compare the experience evoked by the scene vis-à-vis that from her recalled memory. The psychodrama had allowed her to free up her feelings towards her mother through catharsis, gain consciousness of them and adapt herself once more to her interaction with her mother. The scene she re-enacted was close to real life and constituted an externalization of her inner mental agony. In this way she could learn about her relationship with her mother with a deeper perception and acceptance. All these resulted from the manifestations of her spontaneity in the role play.

Through the psychodrama experience Nicole was able to feel which aspects of her memory had kept on living to stir up unpleasantness and which aspects had faded into the distance. To be able to heal her past hurt, she needed to see things in a new way. She acted and invented as she created her own drama. What did not happen was as important as what actually happened in that event. She needed to see what was missing from her own vision. When she saw her mother from a different perspective, her memory profile shifted and she was able to forgive.

The session was concluded with a healing script.

"Now that you have forgiven her, I want you to go back to the same safe place you have chosen for yourself, the forest, with the stream next to you and the sunlight shining through the leaves of the trees. This is the very place you started off in the beginning and where you find peace, security and warmth. This is the healing environment you have earlier chosen for yourself. Stay with the experience. In a moment, imagine yourself standing up and walking along the forest path. As you walk along, you see in front of you a little pond of healing water. Walk slowly towards it. Sit by the edge and dip your feet into it. Feel the coolness of the water. Imagine yourself slowly wading into the pond, immersing yourself in the water, and you feel your whole body soaking in the water of forgiveness, peace and calmness. It is a pool of love and compassion and is the place of serenity that you have been searching for all these years to untie the emotional knot that has made you stuck in your life ... In a moment when you are ready, come back to the here and now. You find yourself coming out of the water as a changed person, and able to start life afresh and leave the past behind."

Before the start of the therapy session, I thought that I had gotten over the event with the associated blame and anger with my mother a decade ago. However, what had just taken place during the session convinced me that it was not the case. I now realized I had been holding back all my pent-up tension all these years.

It was another tiring session, and my eyes were swollen from crying by the time the session ended. Part of my fatigue was contributed by the catharsis. I slowly got off the couch and sat by the consultation table, dazed by my emotions. My head was heavy and my mind was a void. All of a sudden, I heard myself saying, "I think ... I am just a victim of life."

Dr. Mack appeared startled. His eyes widened and I heard him exclaim, "Yes, that is it!"

I turned my head slowly to look at him, and it finally struck me that I had actually been suffering from the victim mentality all these years! Never once before today did I ever see myself from this perspective. My suffering had always seemed justifiable to me. I was surprised when the words came out of my mouth, but I knew it originated from deep within.

It dawned on me that what I had just said was perfectly true! All these years of pain that I had suffered, the blame that I put on others, the frustration, powerlessness and low self-esteem burning within me, had all arisen because I saw myself as a victim. I was a victim of my mother's dominance, a victim of life's circumstances, and a victim of my choice to stay powerless. Being a victim, I had given my power away to everyone else but myself. I had failed to take ownership of steering my life in the direction I wanted.

Thinking over it, this victim identity has cost me many years of misery in my life!

Therapist's Note (6): On Cognitive Restructuring
Dr. Peter Mack

When a patient finds a way of transforming a significant stressor in his life, the transformation is referred to as "cognitive restructuring".

It was a moment of enlightenment when Nicole spontaneously recognized that the concept of "victim mentality" was an appropriate description of her. Nicole's sense of herself being a victim all this while had been preventing her from making objective evaluations and decisions. As a child, she grew up under the care of a domineering mother and her core physical and emotional needs were not met. Unconsciously, she had developed the attitude of looking to others instead of to herself for emotional fulfillment. She had developed a set of beliefs about her ability to cope successfully with adverse circumstance. Having been reliant on others for her comfort, her overly critical mother had unconsciously fostered a sense of her being "not good enough" in her growing years. In her adulthood, she had tended to remain frozen with such a behavioral pattern. It is like a deer which responds to an approaching tiger by standing paralyzed instead of immediately fleeing.

> *"Meditation is not a way of making your mind quiet. It's a way of entering into the quiet that's already there – buried under the 50,000 thoughts the average person thinks every day."*
>
> *Deepak Chopra*

Session 3 (Meditation): Wisdom of "Reversal"

It appeared as if I was going through an epiphany! On the morning of the following day, I took out the new journal book that I had bought recently and designated it as *My Healing Journal*. It was an A5-sized, dark-blue hardcover diary with twin loop-wire ring binding and an elastic book strap. It was a simple journal but I liked it a lot. I caressed the smooth cover, flipped it open to the first page and took a deep breath. I had earlier set my intention to document everything that I experienced during my therapy session, my self-reflection and insights during this crucial period. Then I gripped my pencil and started writing. I described in detail every image and whatever had transpired during the two previous sessions, while the memory was fresh and vivid in my mind.

An hour later, satisfied with my progress, I put down my pencil and looked through what I had written. Then I pondered over the meaning of the story of the princess and the castle for several minutes, but no insights appeared.

"Well, what will come, will eventually come," I reassured myself.

Next I plugged on my earphones, turned on some meditation music and closed my eyes. A tender, calming and meditative mood set in. I decided to commence my meditation for the day.

I took a deep breath and then exhaled slowly, doing my best to focus on my breathing while listening to the soothing background music. Random thoughts started to pop into my mind like before, but I was able to gently distract myself away from them and refocus on my breathing.

Next, I decided to summon the image of my healing forest that I encountered in my therapy session yesterday. The image came on instantly. I saw the trees of the forest, the water in the stream and the beautiful sunlight penetrating the crown canopy and I started to feel more peaceful. My heartbeat and breathing slowed, and so did my brain waves. I felt calm and peaceful.

After a while, I felt more relaxed. Time passed and I decided it was time to conclude my meditation session. I slowly opened my eyes. Suddenly, the word "REVERSAL" appeared in my mind's eye. The next moment, I saw the image of the kind English lady at the cottage, bending over to pass me the bowl of soup, and smiling at me. In the next instant, her face was unexpectedly replaced by my mother's stern face, and my mother was handing over something painful to me instead.

The moment froze, and everything suddenly became clear to me!

The story from my first therapy session was actually meant to be interpreted in *reverse,* both in the storyline's sequence and the characters' traits!

The story started with a young girl, happy and free on the plains. She became sad and lonely after her house was burned down, and chose to seek refuge in a castle for ten years, before deciding to leave for freedom. She finally encountered the warm cottage where a kind and warm lady handed her a much-needed comfort – a bowl of warm soup.

The story paralleled with my current life. It started in reverse at the moment when I realized that the kind English lady handing me an item of comfort was actually my "unkind" mother handing me something painful – the decision to study Medicine.

With the story in reverse sequence, I rode back to the castle, which was the "refuge" for my victim mentality, and chose to trap myself in it for ten years. The castle appeared shiny and safe on the outside, but it was actually empty, cold and lifeless within. I chose to trap myself in it even though I was unhappy, lonely and isolated because I thought it was the only safe place I knew. This part of the story was related to my actual past.

Yet, just as how the young girl had chosen to enter the castle, I could just as well have chosen to leave the place, face the burned house of the past (my painful memories), and leave for the grassland of happiness and freedom that I enjoyed as a young girl. This part was my subconscious mind pointing a way out for me to move ahead in my future!

From the story, I saw how the decision I'd made with regards to my tertiary education had significantly affected me for the past fourteen years. It also revealed the choice I could make henceforth – to start afresh on the plains of happiness and freedom that await me.

How amazing!

I was truly taken aback by this sudden flash of insight. It was a moment of self-realization and the meaning that just felt so right. For the first time in my life, I felt a connection to a higher power, and sensed a bigger presence than myself. I felt something beyond what my five senses could account for.

I could not contain my excitement at unraveling the mystery of the story! This was one of the most profound experiences I'd had since the start of the therapy. I felt connected to my deeper self, a self that was at peace, and to which my heart had opened with love. I immediately documented the insights in my journal, and proceeded to inform Dr. Mack of this moment of manifestation of self-truth that I found so inspiring!

Therapist's Note (7): On Psychic Gestation
Dr. Peter Mack

An epiphany is a flash of insight characterized by a moment of "Ah-ha" clarity. There is an acute awareness of something new which the individual has previously been blind to. There are three components of an epiphany: (1) the setup, as represented by the regression story of the princess and the castle which allowed Nicole to misunderstand the meaning behind the situation; (2) the trigger, which is the meditative event that revealed to Nicole her erroneous interpretation; and (3) the moment, during which the word "REVERSAL" flashed in her mind and enabled her to discern the truth through a backward sequence of the storyline. The flash of illumination made it possible for her to get past an impasse and experience a change in self-identity. While the actual insight in such a situation may be momentary, the resulting personal transformation can be long-lasting.

Over the course of the two days, Nicole had intuitively pieced the fragments of her metaphoric narrative together and allowed the emergence of a newly synthesized understanding of herself. Her healing process had been rapid since. She had suffered from a lot of psychological pain, inner imbalance and a lack of meaning for years. Her diverse inner elements were disconnected with each other. When these elements subsequently came together and emerged as a series of greater wholes, she experienced a sudden surge of energy, sense of wellbeing and an increased depth of meaning in her life.

This "Ah-ha" moment illustrates the fact that the objective of regression therapy is not just for elimination of negative emotions. Rather it aims at evoking wholeness in the individual so as to bring about a new and broader frame of reference in the inner psyche. The process may be regarded as a form of "psychic gestation", one that has a close analogy with biological gestation.

Psychic gestation occurs in the depths and recesses of the unconscious mind while its biological counterpart happens in the mystery of the mother's womb. Both processes are autonomous functions and both terminate with a climax in the miracle of birth. A new life had emerged for Nicole as her "birth" took place. She realized that this new life was possible only because she had activated forces that were already present within her inner self.

CHAPTER TWO

Self-Empowerment

Dr. Nicole Lee

"Manifesting is a lot like making a cake. The things needed are supplied by you, the mixing is done by your mind and the baking is done in the oven of the universe."

Stephen Richards
In: Think Your Way to Success

Synchronicity seemed to be at work. One of my relatives who knew of my interest in Finance passed me a contact of a hedge fund manager, named Robert, a few days after my second therapy session. She thought I could perhaps benefit from learning more about the industry from this man. I was not sure how helpful he might be, but decided to contact him nevertheless.

Robert was responsive and friendly, and we arranged to meet up two days later. As it turned out, what I learned from him about his personal life was astounding. In fact what he told me that day shook me to the core.

Similar to what happened to me, Robert was forced by his parents, in his earlier life, to study something he had no interest in. He wanted to study Gaming Technology, but his parents forced him into Accountancy so that he could become the accountant for the family business. In obedience, he studied four years overseas and obtained his degree. Then he became an auditor at one of the big accountancy firms, a job I thought was no less grueling than being a doctor.

However, unlike me, Robert took matters into his own hands after that. He went on to obtain his CFA certification, a Master in Computer Science and a Diploma in Gaming Technology, all within the three years while working full time at the auditing firm, a feat that seemed impossible to me!

"My parents can force me to study accountancy, but they cannot take my passion away from me," he said to me.

In the course of our conversation, I realized he had no such word as "victimhood" in his dictionary. He worked hard and fought for what he wanted for himself. It was the clearest possible message that the universe had sent me so far. I knew that I could take matters into my own hands from this moment onwards. There would be no more feeling of being victimized and blaming my poor mother for it!

Session 4 (Regression): The Chinese Scholar

A week had passed since my last therapy session. There had been a significant improvement in my mood and I was pleased with the progress.

As I thought over things, I still had many unresolved issues and unanswered questions, chief of which was my purpose in life. I was looking forward to what would be in store for me in the next regression session.

It was the afternoon of 28 May. I arrived at the clinic slightly earlier than usual, but I noticed that Dr. Mack was already waiting for me. By now, I had become more familiar with the therapy process and for this session, I set the intention of addressing the issue of my life purpose. After an initial breathing exercise, I slipped readily into trance.

"As you drift deeper into your hypnotic state, focus on the issue of your life purpose. As you concentrate on the issue, go back to the last time when you were perplexed with it and grappling with the answer. Then allow an emotion to emerge."

A surge of sadness came on, but this sad feeling differed from that of my previous regression session. It was related more to the failure of my hopes.

"Disappointment," I said.

"Focus on the disappointment, and as you do so, I want you to amplify this emotion." Next I heard a count of one to ten, and with every count that Dr. Mack made, I felt an increase in the intensity of my disappointment. On reaching my peak level, I was given the suggestion that this emotion would function as the bridge that would connect myself with a relevant event of the past. Next, I heard a backward count, "Ten, nine, eight ..." When the count of one was reached, an image of ancient China emerged spontaneously.

I was excited! I realized I could possibly be back in a past life. I allowed some time to embody myself into the scene and started to talk.

"I see a young Chinese man in his early twenties. He is a poor scholar and his clothes are old. He is wearing a dull-gray, one-piece clothing with straw shoes. The setting is in one of the ancient Chinese dynasties, but I am not sure exactly which. He is looking at a notice board with a list of names of successful candidates, but his name is not there."

The scene was that of a crowd of Chinese scholars waiting to see the release of the results of the civil service exam that had just taken place. In Imperial China, it was their system to select candidates for the state bureaucracy according to the candidates' level of knowledge of Chinese classics and literary style. Technical expertise was not part of the assessment. Apparently this young man did not make it to the passing list, as revealed by his sad countenance.

"How did he feel when he cannot find his name?"

"Disappointed. His head is hung and I can sense his deep disappointment. He has failed again to pass the exam and this is the third time he has failed. He is sad and extremely disheartened, because he does not have enough money to do it again. He has spent a good part of his life studying but all his efforts have come to nothing. He does not know where to go from here."

> **Therapist's Note (8): The Affect Bridge**
> **Dr. Peter Mack**

The affect bridge is a technique of connecting a relaxed but conscious patient directly with a past event. As the name suggests, the technique uses an affect or emotion to link up two events in which the same emotion is present on both occasions.

Nicole was "moved" experientially from the present to a past incident over a disappointed feeling that was common to both occasions. The current affect of disappointment was identified and vivified with the help of a verbal count from one to ten. She was then asked to return to an earlier experience during which the same affect was experienced. The connecting process drew her into a trance state simultaneously. The bridge connected her all the way back to a past life in ancient China.

The reader may have noted that a similar technique has been used in Session 2, but the connecting emotion used for that occasion was that of "sadness of loss".

"Who are you in relation to this man?"

"I am his wife. I see myself dressed in an old and faded red-colored dress with red shoes made of cloth. I am looking at him now. His eyes are downcast and he looks very dejected. I walk up to him and hold his hands gently in a comforting manner. He looks at me with sadness. We both know that he is not going to attempt the exam anymore."

"What are your emotions then?"

"I feel love for him. I know he has done his best, and there is nothing more we can do. That is the last attempt for him to pass the exam as all our savings have been used up. It is sad that we are in such circumstances, but both of us are resigned to our fate. We walk back to our house. It is a tired-looking wooden hut with a straw roof. We are poor and could barely make ends meet. There are just the two of us in the house. We sit down in silence for a long time at the table. Then he tells me it is time to move on. We are going to move back to the farm where he came from."

"How do you respond to him?"

"I know it is inevitable. So I agree."

At this point, I was guided to the next significant event of this past life. As the scene changed, an image of a rice farm appeared.

"We are at the farm now. We are both farmers. A long day has just ended."

"What have you been doing?"

"Harvesting rice. We are tired, but I can tell we are happier. I wipe off the sweat from his brow. We head back to our house. Our present house is bigger than and not as bare as the previous one. Oh ... I see a young boy running around happily in the house. He is our son!" I was surprised at seeing the image of the young boy.

"How old is the boy?"

"Four to five years of age."

"What are your emotions at this stage?"

A sense of serenity pervaded. "Contented," I replied. "I could sense that we love the boy very much, and we are happy. Life is a lot simpler then. I am preparing a meal at the table, and asking everyone to sit down and eat. The three of us sit at the table for dinner, and use our chopsticks to place food in each other's bowls. Our son cannot handle the chopsticks well and we laugh. We feel happy and contented."

"Look at the boy and see if he is someone you know in your current life?"

I turned to look closely at the boy, but there is no sense of familiarity. So I replied in the negative.

For a second time, I was directed to move on to another significant event. The image of the boy dissolved and when the next scene faded in, I was stunned!

"I see my son's motionless body on the grass ... He is dead! There is a visible snake bite on his left calf. He has been poisoned by a snake! I collapse onto the ground and hug his lifeless body, weeping from the depths of my being. I cannot believe he has died ... It is heartbreaking to see his dead body. We love him so much!"

At this point I could really feel the grief of the loss. It was as if I had really lost my own son. The mounting pain and agony was wrecking my body. It was too much to withstand. I broke down crying and went into catharsis.

"What has happened? How did he get bitten?"

"He was playing by himself in the fields. We do not know what happened until we got back," I replied, struggling with my tears.

"How old is the boy when he died?"

"Five. I see the anguish on my husband's face as tears roll down his cheeks. He blames himself for not passing the exams. Otherwise we would never have had to move back to the fields and our son would not have died ... I do not know how to console him. My own heart is bleeding. I am dazed. I cannot believe what has happened. I sit on the ground for a long, long time, hugging my son's lifeless body."

At this point, Dr. Mack paused for a couple of minutes to allow me to get over my catharsis.

"What happens next?"

"We bury our son. The two of us are standing before his grave, numb from the pain and sorrow. There seems to be a rift between us. Nothing will ever be the same now that our dear son is gone. I see my husband sitting at the table drinking alcohol. He looks unkempt and dazed. Since that day, all he does every day is to drink ... I know it hurts, but I just don't know what to do with him. There is no more joy in the house. Life has become bleak."

I felt the discomfort and heaviness in my heart as the imagery of my depressed husband played out in my mind. Fortunately the scene moved on.

"My husband is forty years of age now and is sick, lying on the bed. I think he is dying."

"What is he suffering from?"

"I don't know. We do not have money for a doctor. He is just very weak and lying on a bed."

"How do you feel?"

"I feel tired. I do not blame him anymore because I know he has been suffering too, since that fateful day. I am not very sad that he is dying, because I see it as a release for him from all his years of guilt and anguish. I also blame myself for not taking better care of our child. So the self-blame all these years has drawn us apart. He holds my hands and says: 'I am sorry for the misery in this life.' Then he draws his last breath."

"How do you feel when he says, 'I am sorry'?"

I sighed on hearing the question.

"I feel very empty. There is no more blame; just emptiness inside, but I still love him. I think it is better for him to move on than to lead such a life. I just hold his hands until he closes his eyes." I paused for a moment and continued, "He has passed on."

"Describe your feelings to me."

"It is a painful life; full of hardship. The only joy has been taken away from us. Life could have been so different. We were poor but we were happy with the child. My husband would not have become like that." My tears started to flow again, as I was describing my feelings.

At the next event, I saw myself at a much older age. "I am staying alone, and I am seventy years of age. My hair is all white."

"What are you doing now?"

"I am sitting alone in the house at the table, looking at the rice fields. I feel a lot more peaceful. But it has been a lonely life after my husband died thirty years ago. I still grieve for our son."

"Mull over your life at this point and tell me if you have fulfilled your life purpose?"

"I wish I was literate, because things might have turned out differently. I could have found other ways to make a living besides farming or needlework, and provided a better environment for our son to grow up."

"Looking back, were there any parts of this past life that you find fulfilling and were happy with?"

"I do not regret marrying my husband. I just wish our child had not died as this life would have been very different, but I cannot change what had happened. When I look back, I keep thinking how different it would have been if the child had not died. That was all I could think of."

I sighed again.

"After my husband died, I spent years by myself. It was just a state of bare existence. I was not depressed but I was not happy either."

At the next scene, I saw myself sitting on my bed coughing out blood onto my palms."

"My time is up," I mumbled.

"What are you suffering from?"

"No idea. There is still no money to see a doctor."

"Is there anybody next to you?"

"I think there are some neighbors, but the image is not very clear. I am not afraid of dying. I know it is time to go."

"Let me move you to the point when your heart stops beating."

Upon hearing Dr. Mack's instructions, I sensed myself leaving the woman's body. There was no fear or anxiety, just a gradual sense of detachment, and increasing lightness. As I turned around to gaze at her lifeless body, a sense of empathy and compassion flooded my being.

Next, I felt my energies separating from the lady's body, and I knew that I was no longer her, from this point on.

"I see myself floating above her. She is an old lady, about seventy years old. Her hair is all white and she is hunched-back. She is lying on her side on the bed. She has died."

"As you are floating above her, are there any thoughts on your mind?"

"She has led a hard life, but she is a strong woman. She endured each day, and made an honest living even though it was lonely. I respect her for her strength and courage to carry on living through the darkest and bleakest days. It is a sad state that she led such a hard life. When I look at her, I can feel my heart aching for her. I feel love and respect for her as well."

Therapist's Note (9): The Death Point
Dr. Peter Mack

Experiencing the death point is a very important part of the regression process. Almost all patients find this a peaceful instead of a fearful process. The first thing the patient notices is usually that he is floating above the physical body or standing beside it. Frequently the individual experiences a replay of his entire life's feelings and emotions as a flashback. However the overall experience is generally one of warmth, comfort and a feeling of being free.

The crossing over to the spirit realm is a move to a loving, light-filled environment and can be facilitated by the therapist. It is in the spirit realm where he can meet his spirit guide, loved ones or whoever has had a significant impact on his life, and resolve any doubts or unfinished business.

"Have all your energies left your body?"

"Yes."

Next I was told I was being brought to the spirit realm. This sounded unfamiliar to me, but I flowed with the instructions nonetheless.

The image of the body of the old lady faded away while I sensed my soul floating upwards, feeling lighter and lighter. I finally stopped in an open space. Intuitively I knew I had arrived at the spirit realm.

At this point, Dr. Mack instructed, "At the spirit realm, seek out your spirit guide for this life and see if they are there."

Instantly, the image of a lady standing upright against a white, misty background started to emerge. She had long hair with a central parting but I could not make out her facial features. She wore a plain white dress with a V-neck opening but there were no patterns in the waistline or pleats.

"There's a lady with long black hair in a white robe appearing before me," I said. "I do not recognize her."

"Speak to her and ask who she is."

The word "Lily" popped into my mind instantly.

"She says she is my spirit guide for this life. Her name is Lily."

"Ask your guide what is the purpose of your current life?"

I paused and waited for Lily's response. "She just says the word 'power'."

"What do you understand that to mean?"

Suddenly, the word "self-empowerment" appeared in my mind's eye.

"It is about self-empowerment, but … I am not getting the full picture of the meaning yet."

"Ask her to elaborate on how self-empowerment will help you fulfill the purpose of your life?"

To my surprise, Lily did not give a direct response. Instead, she reversed the question to me: "In contrast to your past life in China, you are now empowered in your present life with the literacy the woman had craved for. Ask yourself if you have made full use of it?"

Dumbfounded, I was silent for a moment. Then I gave my guide a smile. Lily smiled back gently. We both know the truth. I definitely had not made full use of the intellectual assets that I had been endowed with in my current life, so far. I thanked her for the guidance and bade her farewell.

Dr. Mack brought me out of the spirit realm and concluded the session.

Therapist's Note (10): Purpose of Life
Dr. Peter Mack

What is seldom realized is that each of our individual souls has drawn up a Life Plan for us before we undergo reincarnation. In other words, the soul has decided in advance on the best social and physical environment for the individual to learn the spiritual lesson that he has planned for himself on Earth.

When Nicole was confronted with difficulties in career and a challenging daughter-mother relationship, these were probably the very facets of her life that her soul has planned for her as a life-lesson to learn from. Accordingly, if her relationship with her mother and her career were at the root of her suffering, it was her soul who had incorporated these into her Life Plan. She might have believed that she was poorly suited for a medical career, but from the soul perspective, it was the best possible environment for nurturing her spiritual growth.

I opened my eyes, and everything seemed blurry for a moment. I blinked away the last few drops of tears and pondered over what I had just experienced. I realized that despite being empowered with the intellectual tools to achieve whatever I wanted in this current life, I had yet to utilize it fully. While Lily had not provided an answer to my question on my life purpose the way I expected, she had set me thinking. It was the spiritual message behind what she said that constituted the waking call I needed.

In addition, venturing into the spirit realm and meeting my spiritual guide for the first time was a particularly intriguing experience. It had never struck me before that there were helpers from "the other side" who were literally a thought away and from whose support and guidance I could benefit.

As I emerged fully, a series of questions came to mind.

"Who are spiritual guides and where do they come from?" I could not help blurting out the question, as I was feeling intrigued and fascinated.

Seizing the opportunity, I came up with a further series of questions for Dr. Mack. "What is the soul? Who is my Higher Self? And what are the relationships between my Higher Self, the soul and the One Divine?" These were terms that I had picked up from my own reading some years ago but never fully comprehended. It felt good that there was finally someone I could pose these questions to.

Dr. Mack took a deep breath, gave a chuckle and slowly formulated the answer to my questions. Equally intriguing was the way he constructed his response. Aware of my atheism, he chose to construct his response on the basis of a non-religious framework. It so turned out that his explanation was something I had never encountered before, despite my broad reading interest and passion with spiritual literature. I was thoroughly fascinated!

CHAPTER THREE

Guides, Soul and Higher Self

Dr. Peter Mack

"We are not human beings on a spiritual journey. We are spiritual beings on a human journey."
Pierre Teilhard de Chardin
In: Le Phénomène Humain

Intrigued by the regression experience of crossing the death point and over to the spirit realm, Nicole had emerged from her trance state with some burning questions.

"What are spirit guides?" she wondered, "and where do they come from?" This question immediately spiraled me into deep thought, with regards to the strategy of constructing the reply. For someone who had just gone through a stirring psycho-spiritual experience, I expected she would need a more structured concept to ground her healing experience.

What are Spirit Guides?
In essence, spirit guides are incorporeal beings that are assigned to us to help, protect and guide us through life. They are from a different plane of human existence, occasionally referred to as "the other side". They serve as a mediator between the world of being and nonbeing and help us to fulfill the spiritual contract we make with ourselves before we reincarnate.

When a patient is under a state of altered consciousness, his mind is able to connect with the wider cosmic consciousness and recognize his spirit guide through guided imagery. Under trance, spirit guides can appear in many forms, and therapists conveniently enlist their assistance in their patients' healing process. Frequently, when the patient under trance has been regressed through the death point in a past life and experienced his soul's departure from the physical body, it takes little added effort on the part of the therapist to direct the soul energy into the spirit realm. By subtly integrating the soul's subsequent interaction with his guide into his past life experience, valuable answers and insights to the individual's life issues can often be obtained.

Functionally, spirit guides play the role of a mentor or teacher whenever we connect with them. They guide us on our journey in between the conscious and the unconscious worlds and function as our personal advisors and stay with us from birth to death. Some of them will come and go, and change according to our needs and level of spiritual growth. There are yet others who are assigned to us for a specific period of time to help us to learn specific lessons.

Spirit guides are beings with positive energy and their only concern for us is our higher good. When they come and go, they guide as well as protect us. They help us with remembering who we are, letting go of our fears and learning to love ourselves and others. They assist us in making our own choices in life, building a broader sense of awareness, and facilitate our personal growth. Along the way, they also provide the necessary support in developing our inner strength and deeper wisdom.

A consistent feature of these guides is their paucity of remarks. They are not here to lead and direct. They tend to convey wisdom with few words. Hence they often deliver answers in the form of hints and messages. Sometimes the messages come through signs, symbols and metaphors because these are the most direct mode of getting in touch with our subconscious mind. They teach love and forgiveness and their advice is never self-serving. They always attend to our request for information, but will not communicate or intervene without our permission.

Spirit guides are composed of pure energy and can manifest in many ways, from the more primal forms, as flashes of light or feelings of love, to the more familiar forms with human appearances. As the later chapters will reveal, Nicole's guides have come in two human forms, one in each gender, and there is an important reason for this duality.

The ultimate role of a spirit guide is to help us to accomplish what we have come here to do on Earth. He assists us to fulfill our "karmic purpose". What we have done or not done in our previous lives determines our karma. Our sacred contract is based on our karmic lessons and how best to use these lessons to prepare ourselves to accomplish our greater purpose in the current lifetime on Earth.

Nature of the Soul

The understanding of the concept of the soul is complex and is based on a variety of human capacities and experiences. These include our interpretations of life and death, and our experiences with dreaming, intuition, inspiration, near-death experience, out-of-body experience and various mystical experiences.

The soul concept has evolved significantly over the centuries.[5] In the earliest phase, the soul, in its primitive form, is believed to be in a quasi-physical reality of some kind, such as a vapor, body or light. As thinking evolves, the concept incorporated certain psychological qualities. This includes desire, thought, passion, will and self-consciousness, and personality. In the more recent development of thought, the concept adds on the idea of a connection with a divine reality.

Added to the confusion is that the term is being used in many ways by different people. Its use has been unconsciously influenced by Biblical literature and the works of early Greek philosophers. It is further complicated by inevitable changes in meaning when religious and philosophical content is translated

---

[5] The evolution of the soul concept is described in *Shadow, Self, Spirit: Essays in Transpersonal Psychology* by Michael Daniels, 2005.

from one language to another. For example, in the Bible, the term has been used with four different meanings: (i) a person; (ii) a form of life that a man possesses but ceases to exist upon death; (iii) a person's emotions and inner thoughts; and (iv) the immortal part of a person. Added to this is the church's teaching that the soul is what connects us to God and that we must keep our souls pure by following the morals of the Bible.

In a non-Biblical context, however, the term soul is used in everyday speech, to represent various ideas, such as the vital principle in man, the seat of feelings and sentiments, the innermost part of ourselves or the moral aspect of man.

> *"When you do things from your soul, you feel a river moving in you, a joy."*
>
> *Rumi*

In regression therapy, the soul is interpreted as the deepest part of one's consciousness. It is the source of our individual awareness and is made up of pure spirit energy that contains memories and experiences gathered in our physical incarnations. In each incarnation the individual soul has its lessons to learn, often involving getting along with others, loving and forgiving them. As a result it grows in wisdom with each life experience. It interacts with other souls at different stages of its cosmic journey and creates karma as it becomes entangled in the consequences of its actions with other souls in its different lives.

Hence, as individuals in our current life, we are likened to rivers. On the surface we all appear clear and shiny, but running deep within us are unseen currents. These currents are our soul memories and desires. They are made up of the cumulative effects of the experience of many incarnations on Earth. The role of the soul in reincarnation is given in more detail in Appendix II.

Higher Self

The Higher Self is an even more difficult concept to define. It characterizes an eternal omnipotent and intelligent being who is one's true self, and this has been featured prominently in certain forms of psychotherapy.[6] It is regarded as an extension of one's worldly self into a more advanced and incorporeal realm. Very often, it is regarded as a form of being which is recognized as existing in a union with a divine source. Surprisingly, the imagery of the Higher Self is easy to take shape during an altered state of consciousness, as Nicole herself can testify.

For some people the term Higher Self is used interchangeably with the *True Self, Real Self, Innermost Self, Spiritual Self* or *Transpersonal Self*. The general concept is that the Higher Self contains an advanced source of insight into man's most vexing questions, such as one's existential purpose, the meaning of life and death, etc. Many practitioners of meditation have experienced a consistent outcome of acquisition of peace and intuition when making a connection with their Higher Self. Once in the meditative state they are able to tap into their higher intelligence through their Higher Selves and develop a more enlightened perspective on existential issues.

One Divine

I believe the so-called "One Divine" as mentioned by Nicole (Chapter 6) refers to the Principle of Unity or the Law of One. It is a reminder that there is only one Consciousness. Each of our individual consciousness is a special facet of the one Consciousness of all things. It is the awareness that all is one, and all souls are cells of this body of awareness.

When the Law of One is observed, there is no need for any of us to struggle and compete, because competition is akin to our body parts fighting each other and the body being at war with itself (Chapter 11). When we understand the principle of oneness and the totality of the universe, all that appears separate will become an illusion, and all of us will move into universal harmony.

---

[6] Psychosynthesis as developed by Roberto Assagioli is an approach to psychotherapy that features the Higher Self prominently.

We are all part of the universe or the Divine, and the Divine is in us. What is imperfect is the connection between our conscious and the unconscious, or between our Lower and Higher Self. This is due to the limitation of our lower bodies or vehicles. However this communication can be improved through the quiet habit of one-pointed and sustained concentration via meditation.

In later chapters, Nicole eventually learned that it is a spiritual path that we follow when we get into healing. It is a path in which we explore questions of existence and the ultimate meaning of our relationship to the mysteries of life (Chapter 13). Through our spiritual practice we expose the deepest dimensions of our identity and encounter a force within ourselves, this world that Nicole recognizes as the One Divine.

CHAPTER FOUR

The Path to Spirituality

Dr. Nicole Lee

"Let yourself be drawn by the stronger pull of what you truly love."

Rumi

The discourse on the soul and the spirit world had been most fascinating. In addition to having my doubts and spiritual uncertainties addressed, I had since begun to appreciate the essence of spirituality better. The metaphysical concepts of life and life beyond death had been presented in such a way that I could now appreciate how regression therapy had worked the way it did on me.

However, other questions remained unanswered. What is my calling? Is it the practice of Medicine? Since I have no strong impulse towards any particular course of action, how am I going to know what I should be doing next?

It was the morning of 29 May. The story of the Chinese scholar was still fresh on my mind and I had been mulling over the insights. I had indeed been awakened to the fact that I had not been leveraging on my capacities and the opportunities in my current life. But, in what way should I be making use of my assets and opportunities?

I decided that it was time to continue with the quest on my own.

Session 5 (Meditation): Creating One's Reality

After weeks of practice, I had become familiar with the techniques of achieving mindfulness through sitting meditation. I had also begun to appreciate the importance of paying precise, non-judgmental attention to the details of my experience as they arise and subside, and be with them.

In the quietness of my study, I closed my eyes, and focused my attention on my breath. As I was inhaling slowly but deeply, I told myself that I was breathing in the light of the morning and imagined the light flooding the tissues of my body and touching every cell. Next I breathed out, slowly and in a long-drawn manner. While doing so, I imagined the tension of the body departing together with my exhalation and evaporating under the morning sun. Then I took the next breath in and the cycle continued.

After three deep breaths, the image of the same forest with the stream and rabbits that I saw in Session 2 reappeared in my mind's eye. Seeing it helped me to obtain a focused concentration because I felt I needed a meditation object of some sort to prevent my mind from drifting. Ever since that session, I had embraced it as my personal healing forest. Each time as it appeared at the start of my meditation, I began to feel much more relaxed and peaceful.

As I drifted into the alpha state,[7] I saw a flash of energy in front of me. The image of a lady gradually appeared in my mind screen. I was intrigued, and I reminded myself to stay relaxed and allow the imagery to fully emerge. This lady had short hair, and was dressed in a white robe, similar to the one that Lily wore. She looked just like me and intuitively I knew she was my Higher Self!

At the next moment, a second image gradually appeared. This was Lily, my spirit guide. She was seen standing next to my

---

[7] The brain is electric. As the mind relaxes into a state of effortless alertness, the brain generates electrical waves of 8–12Hz in frequency and these are known as alpha waves.

Higher Self. I was happy to see both of them together and greeted them warmly.

> **Therapist's Note (11): Contacting Spirit Guides**
> **Dr. Peter Mack**
>
> The practice of communicating with spirit guides is as old as civilization itself. It takes desire, practice and a dedication to learn how to go beyond our five senses. The hypnotic or meditative state provides the platform for the communication. It involves an alignment of the energy vibrations of both the guide and the individual's soul for this to be possible.
>
> Spirit guides transmit information to us in different ways, including thoughts, light images or other forms of energy. Frequently their transmissions need interpretation and their images need to be translated into our conceptual framework. Nicole's guide tends to speak to her in metaphorical imagery and this mode is probably most suited to her needs and efficient for getting the message through.
>
> Contact with spirit guides often gives the counsel and recommendations that one can understand and immediately apply. These may be in the form of ideas that we have heard before but now presented in a new way. Sometimes it may be just a trigger word to get the message across (e.g. the word "reversal" in Session 3). The term by itself may have no special meaning to other people but it brings to the individual awareness and association of certain thoughts or ideas that illustrate the communication.

Next I asked them the question that had been bugging me for years. "What is my true calling? What is the vocation that I will find fulfillment in?"

The two of them did not verbalize any answer. Instead they turned around and started walking in the opposite direction away from me and beckoned me to follow. As we were walking deeper into the forest, the vegetation became increasingly dense. I tried catching up with them but their pace was too fast for me. With each step, they were becoming further and further ahead of me.

All of a sudden, I lost sight of both of them and found myself surrounded by the dense forest. I began to feel panicky. My throat tightened up and my heart was pounding hard. I started to shout for help!

In the midst of my anguish, I heard their calming voices echoing through the trees: "*You create your own reality ...*"

My mind stilled. Somehow these words struck a resonance with my inner self and reverberated in my consciousness. As I looked around me now, the surrounding forest suddenly transformed itself into a doctor's clinic! I stared at it for a moment and soon the image of the clinic slowly dissolved and crossfaded into the image of an artist's workroom. I tried to study the details of the art room only to find that the image transition continued. This time it became a trader's office, gradually followed by that of a chef's kitchen.

I stood still and was bewildered; my eyes were transfixed by the continually changing scenes. The images faded, and the next moment, Lily and my Higher Self reappeared in front of me.

"You see, you create your own reality," they said. "You are empowered to create anything you want, or be anyone whom you want to be. There is nothing to stop you."

My mind froze for a moment as I was grasping the truth in a way that transcended word descriptions. It was the kind of knowing that made me look at myself in a brand new way!

"How true ..." I murmured as I nodded to myself.

I finally realized what the meaning of self-empowerment was all about. My true calling was the reality I wanted to create for myself. Only I could create my own reality and the truth was that I was in control of my own destiny all this while. I suddenly understood that I had the power to become who I want to be, no matter what the circumstances. This fundamental truth had suddenly shed light onto my problem. A new world was opening up before me.

At this point I opened my eyes and came out of my meditative state. It was an "Ah-ha" moment.

A renewed source of energy and courage seemed to be flowing into me. I understood that developing an insight was about ridding the chatter from my mind. In fact, much of the chatter in my mind had been born out of my beliefs in self-importance.

After some moments of overwhelming wonder and awe, I closed my eyes again. I lapsed into a meditative state once more. With this new understanding, I decided to seek follow-up advice from the higher beings on my next issue: How to go about making my choice?

"Since I am empowered to be anyone I want to be, and with so many choices at my disposal, what should I choose?" I asked.

My guide Lily and my Higher Self reappeared. This time they stood next to me, one on either side. They remained silent and did not answer my question.

Next, my Higher Self held my left hand while Lily held on to my right hand. At the next moment, I found myself being split into two. At the same time, they said to me, "Choose one of us to follow to find out the truth."

Immediately my mind started to analyze and attempted to rationalize which of the two was a better bet. I felt this was necessary because it was important for me to find the correct person to help me discover the "real" truth. I felt distressed at having to make such an important decision. After much mental struggle I remarked: "I cannot decide! What if I choose to follow one of you and miss something crucial on the other side?"

In the next instant, all three of us were now holding hands in a circle. Lily and my Higher Self said to me: "There are always choices and lost chances. But whatever you choose, it does not matter. *All paths lead to One.*"

The last sentence rang loudly in my ears. There are countless ways of seeking an understanding of the profound mysteries of the universe and there are many paths to the same truth. Some paths might appear longer than the others, but ultimately all paths lead to the One Divine or Consciousness. Therefore the actual choice is less important than the act and intention of making it!

I shivered in excitement and emerged from my meditation. I was amazed at the imagery and messages in this session. They were certainly not something I would have generated for myself in my usual musings.

It had also dawned on me that what had been holding me back in life was my inability to decide. I had been looking for the "real" or "correct" truth each time. Whenever I doubted the correctness of my choice, I would retrace my steps, lapse into indecision and get stuck in the process. This had been happening to many facets of my life, chief of which were the way I stood up to my mother, my choice of career, and my search for the meaning of life.

The message I had obtained from this meditative exercise was to make the choice with a clear intention and move on. My indecisiveness had caused me much distress, lost time and missed opportunities over the years. It was time to move on in my life.

CHAPTER FIVE

Leap of Faith

Dr. Nicole Lee

"Don't fear failure so much that you refuse to try new things. The saddest summary of life contains three descriptions: could have, might have, and should have."
Louise E. Boone

Prior to starting therapy, my life had been stagnant, and I was in a limbo state. Shortly into the therapy, I had started to notice that things began to move without any added effort on my part.

Earlier this year my husband and I had listed our apartment for sale. It was a major decision in our life. We wanted to relocate ourselves because we needed a change in our living environment. However, the local property market outlook was bleak during this period, and prices were falling. After listing our apartment for three months, there were no satisfactory offers. It was disheartening. We discussed and decided to change our mind about selling our property, and our apartment listing had since been taken off.

Two months passed. This was the time when I reconnected with Dr. Mack and made the decision to commence meditation and therapy. One evening, I suddenly received a call from my property agent. A serious buyer was interested in our apartment. He came over the next day, viewed our apartment and, within ten minutes, made an offer to purchase. The price was reasonable and we sold our apartment within three days. Three months of listing our apartment earlier this year and nothing happened! I remarked to my husband that a "special" force was helping us move ahead!

I had since decided to pay attention to every sign and message that the universe and my guides were sending me. Each of these seemed to have come for a specific purpose. I believed that they had either helped me to finalize a decision or confirmed something that I already knew but was uncertain about. Paying attention to them gave me a more confident feeling that I could now live my life in a clearer direction.

Session 6 (Meditation): The Girl in the Ice Land
It was a quiet Friday morning on 30 May, and I was alone at home. I had been very excited over the positive results from my recent meditation exercises so far and wanted to pursue the practice regularly. This time I stated my intention to explore my issues of insecurity, unexplained fear of life, and the associated shame at being so fearful.

I plugged in my earphones, switched on some meditation music, and closed my eyes. A sense of inner calm followed.

Both my spirit guide and my Higher Self had been a wonderful help in moving me towards a waking state of happiness, health and peace. This time, I decided to contact my Higher Self first.

After a short moment of inner calm, my Higher Self appeared in my mind's eye, standing in front me. She was dressed in her usual white, flowing robe. She then held my right hand and signaled me to follow her.

As we walked, a white mist started to envelop us. With each step, the mist grew denser and denser. Finally, I heard her voice telling me to let go of her hand. With some trepidation, I reluctantly loosened my grip, not knowing what to expect next.

The mist cleared.

The next thing I saw were snowflakes falling in front of my eyes. Amazingly, I could make out the fine details of each snowflake and its beautiful pattern and colors as the sunlight refracted through each crystal. Soon, I realized that I was a teenage girl in an ice-capped landscape. The ground was covered with thick snow.

There were a set of footprints in the snow leading away from me. When I laid my fur-lined boots in them, I noticed they matched my size. I followed the footprints, and saw that they ended in front of a circular patch of ice surrounded by the snow. Attracted by curiosity, I walked up to the ice patch and looked into it.

The sight of what I saw stunned me! There was a man's face in the water pressed up against the ice! In that instant, I sensed fragmented images of him struggling in the water, and he eventually stopped moving. I jolted to my senses and immediately picked up an ice pick nearby and started hacking at the ice. The ice cracked. I quickly gained access to the man, tied a rope around his limp body, and pulled him out with all my strength. His body was cold. I hit his chest hard several times to revive him. Just as I was about to give up, he coughed and sputtered out water. He was still alive! I breathed a sigh of relief. Next I saw myself supporting his weak body as we walked back to a cottage.

At this point, there was a sudden flash of new knowledge in my mind. He was my stepfather in that lifetime and I was the one who had earlier tried to drown him by pushing him into the icy water! I was taken aback. For a moment, I could not come to terms with this new awareness, and the scene came to a standstill.

I then took a deep breath to refocus my mind. As I breathed out, I allowed the mental clutter to be expelled with the exhalation. After repeating this cycle twice, the images reappeared and slowly, the entire story became clear.

Starting with a quick flashback of myself being a baby in my mother's arms, I saw my mother and myself being thrown out of her house for some reason. A man rescued us. He fell in love with my mother and subsequently became my stepfather, and we came to live in the cottage that I saw in the earlier segment of my meditation.

At the next scene, I saw myself as a young girl living and growing up in the cottage. I was looking at my mother and stepfather hugging each other and could sense their deep loving bond. As I watched them, I felt my resentment and jealousy at their closeness. They were not unkind to me, but I felt like an outsider, redundant, unloved and insecure.

One day, I saw my mother carrying a bucket of clothes to wash at a river a distance from the house. I was still a young girl then. I was bored, and I decided to follow a few meters behind her, and she was unaware of my presence. Suddenly, a large bear appeared and attacked her! The bucket fell to the ground, and the clothes were strewn all over the snow. At this moment, I felt myself as emotionlessly watching the fatal attack from behind a tree. I did not run for help. Soon, there was blood all over the snow-covered ground. I watched my mother die with indifference.

My stepfather was deeply saddened by my mother's death. He did not know that I had witnessed the attack and yet did not run for help. Since then, he raised me on his own. Although he was not unkind, he became more aloof and cold. I resented him, and started to plot his demise, in the belief that it would free me from my existing unhappiness.

At the next scene, I saw myself holding a fishing rod, resting it on my left shoulder, heading out of the house into the snow. My stepfather was walking beside me, carrying other fishing equipment. We reached a frozen ice pond. I hacked open a small area of ice and dropped my fishing line in. I watched him from the corner of my eyes as he put down the equipment and busied himself with his fishing task. The next thing I knew, I had crept up stealthily behind him and pushed him into the water!

After my stepfather recovered from the near-drowning at home, he calmly told me to pack my belongings and leave the house. He knew I had attempted to drown him. I kept silent and did not plead with him. I packed my bag, held my head high and stepped out into the snow, hiding the overwhelming fear within me.

As I went further and further away from the house I started to cry. There was an endless stretch of white snow in front of me. I started to tremble as I finally realized the situation I had landed myself in. The warm tears rolled down my frozen cheeks and my vision was blurred. I had nowhere to go.

The last image I saw was the dead body of the girl. After being attacked by a pack of wolves, she died in a pool of her own blood in the snow. The meditative story ended here. While there were themes of insecurity, fear and shame in the story, I was unfortunately unable to discern a deeper message.

Next my Higher Self and Lily appeared in front of me. I asked them how this story addressed the issue of my pervasive sense of insecurity. They both remained silent.

Next, Lily led me to a well. Then she told me to look into it. I saw the water in the well whirlpool downwards until the well was empty. Next moment, I found myself at the bottom of the well and looking up at the circular view of the sky. The phrase "frog at the bottom of a well" came into my mind.

I shouted for help to get out. A voice told me to crawl out by myself. I clawed at the stone walls of the well but I failed to obtain any grip. Finally, I shouted: "Throw me a rope!"

A rope dropped down the side of the stone wall. I held on to it and climbed out of the well. On reaching the top I saw Lily standing by the side of the well, and I asked her what did all this mean? She smiled, and said nothing. Again, I was none the wiser.

At the next instant, Lily waved her arm and the well disappeared. I saw myself now lying on the soft grass in my healing forest, next to a stream, and with sunlight streaming through the canopy of the leaves. It was peaceful and tranquil as usual. This time, I saw two cute little bunnies in my forest, and they snuggled close to me.

Next to me was a row of forest trees. I noticed a swing hanging by a rope from one of the branches of the biggest tree in the forest. It was not there before and now it was dangling down by my side. I merrily walked up to the swing, sat on it and started to swing. The little bunnies hopped over to watch me, and their heads bobbed up and down with each oscillation. "How adorable!" I remarked to myself, and I smiled.

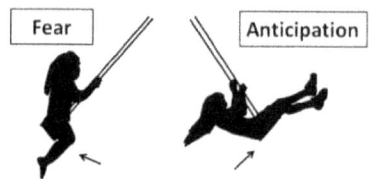

The swinging motion soon picked up momentum. The arc got wider and the seat of the swing went higher and higher. At the extreme end of the oscillation when I was facing forwards and downwards, I experienced fear. There was an uncontrollable tingling sensation in my body at the thought of the impending descent. After the swing went past the neutral point and was near to the upper end of the opposite extreme, I felt the anticipation of the impending descent backwards. I was swinging between fear and anticipation.

At this stage, Lily and my Higher Self appeared in front of me again. They smiled and said, "Do you see? This swing is analogous to your life. The higher you swing, the more fear and anticipation you gather. You fear your life so much not because you are a coward, but because you anticipate so much for it too. *The greater your anticipation, the greater is your fear.* There is nothing to be ashamed of." Their words swept right into my consciousness. There was a sudden and abrupt insight. My self-concept was transformed instantly.

I started to cry.

"I am not a coward! There is nothing to be ashamed of!" I repeated those words to myself. "I fear so much because I have a zest for life more than I ever realized! Now I know!"

I got off the swing and walked up to them, feeling immensely grateful for their words of wisdom. The years of uncertainty that I had gone through, riddled with fear and self-blame, were finally over. They ended, all with a simple metaphor – the swing!

"How does all this relate to my insecurity issue?" I asked.

Again, there was no verbal response. However, in the next instant, the rope from which the swing had been hanging suddenly snapped, first on one side and then the other. The swing fell to the ground.

> **Therapist's Note (12): On Metaphors**
> Dr. Peter Mack
>
> The essence of a metaphor is the understanding and experiencing of one idea or concept in terms of another. When we accept the fact that most of our thought processes go beyond our conscious understanding, metaphors give a unique perspective into how we think, feel and experience the world around us. Using metaphors is one way of deciphering our unconscious wisdom.
>
> The use of metaphors in healing involves an interaction between the intellect, the imagination and the emotions. The unconscious mind does not think in literal terms but processes information in terms of relationships and patterns. The tenor and the vehicle interact in such a way that new meaning is produced.
>
> The swing resembles Nicole's life because the extremes of the oscillating motion connect with her cognitive and behavioral patterns. In the process of resemblance, similarity is perceived. Because two formerly distant realities now appear closely related, new meaning is created. Under trance, Nicole has a sense of herself being present in the world of abstract imagination where the swing metaphor tells her that she has been living her life in a way that is problematic.

I looked at the broken swing, paused and shook my head helplessly. I was perplexed.

Lily and my Higher Self then pointed to the branch from which the swing was hanging. At that moment I saw branches of different calibers, some thick and sturdy, while others were thin and fragile.

"Would you get on the swing if you know that the branch is fragile?" they asked.

"Certainly not! No one would," I replied.

"What if the branch is hidden and covered by leaves, and there is no way of knowing whether it is thick or thin? Will you forever stand in front of the swing and wonder what the risk is like to swing on it, or will you get on the swing anyway?"

I pondered for a moment and replied, "I will get on the swing eventually, and probably out of curiosity."

"There you are." They smiled and said, *"There is no such thing as security in life.* You will never know whether the branch is sturdy or fragile before you swing on it. It is just like many circumstances in life where you will never know beforehand the consequences of the different actions you can possibly take.

"Even if the branch does snap, and you fall to the ground as a result, only two things will happen. Either you get hurt, pull yourself together and move on, or you die from the fall and move on to the next lifetime. Either way, it does not matter. *All that matters is the leap of faith. It is for you to take that leap to experience your life fully*."

Their words echoed in my mind. There is no such thing as security in life! I now realized that the image of the snapping ropes and broken swing was meant to remind me of the absence of security in life.

In the next instant, the scene changed and the three of us were sitting on the ground facing each other. I expressed my gratitude to them again for helping me to unravel my doubt after all these years.

Instantly, at this point I understood how the ice-land story would relate to my insecurity and fear issues:

Therapist's Note (13): Structural Mapping in Metaphors
Dr. Peter Mack

A metaphor is a mechanism whereby one experiential domain at source is partially mapped and projected onto another experiential domain so that the second domain is understood in terms of the first. A patient's metaphor often reveals a great deal about his major concerns, interpersonal relationships and his perceptions of self and others.

The metaphor creates new meaning by finding similarities and mapping the knowledge from the base to the target. The premise is that the system of relations that holds for the base objects (the swing) also holds among the target objects (life decisions). Firstly, there is an initial process of symmetric alignment in which the swing hanging from a weakened tree branch is put in correspondence with the risks that one faces in life as an analogy. Secondly, the process goes through a phase in which the inferences are projected onto the target. The decision-making mode derived from the "broken-swing dilemma" is now projected onto the life act of trusting in something that cannot be readily seen or proved.

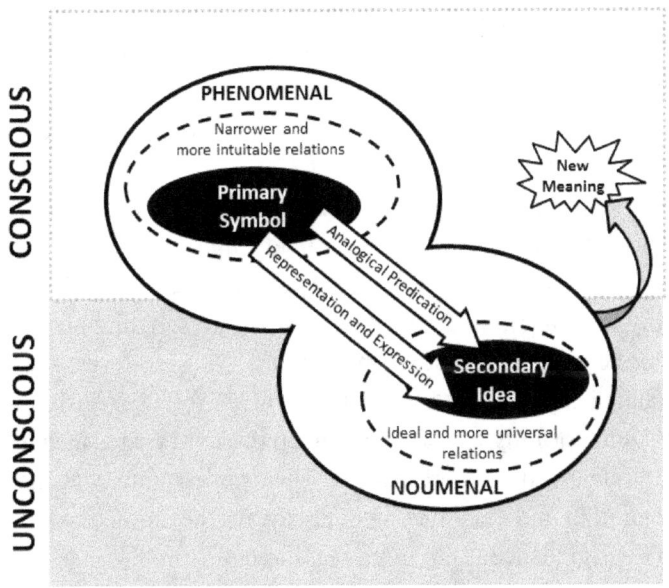

The Girl at the Ice Land – In this story I was envious and jealous of the love and closeness between my mother and stepfather. Because of this envy and jealousy, I distanced myself from them, and in the process also failed to love myself. There was a fear that I could become redundant in their lives one day. All these negative emotions – envy, jealousy, lack of self-love, and fear of redundancy, led to my insecurity, and ultimately my evil nature that let me watch my mother die with indifference, and plot the death of my stepfather.

Likewise in my current life, I am experiencing insecurity because of my envy of other people's successes, made worse by the lack of self-love and self-worth. Over the years, I had increasingly taken on a negative view of human nature, and as a result I had become self-defensive and began to distance myself from others. I knew if I did not change this worldview soon, my negative patterns would overwhelm me eventually.

The Frog in the Well – As for the well, Lily subsequently showed me the perspective from above the well when I was still below and inside the well. Unknown to me, as I could not see the happenings above the well from the bottom, I was actually the one next to Lily, who had thrown the rope down to rescue my other self below!

From my perspective at the bottom of the well, I was under the impression that the rope came from either Lily or my Higher Self, but it was not. Now I had learned the lesson – all I needed to get out of my little world in the well was to help myself, and be ready to ask for help and accept it when it comes.

I thanked my Higher Self and Lily again for their insightful help. I could not fully express how much these messages meant to me, but I knew they were aware. They smiled and gave me a wave and told me that they would always be around when I needed their guidance. I felt more reassured.

My meditation session ended. I opened my eyes, and everything stayed surreal for a moment. It was truly amazing. Being rational by nature, I knew there was no way my conscious self could have come up with all these messages and metaphorical stories on my own.

CHAPTER SIX

Envy and Jealousy

Dr. Nicole Lee

"Do not overrate what you have received, nor envy others. He who envies others does not obtain peace of mind."

Gautama Siddharta

To date, the messages and directions from my spirit guide and Higher Self to me had come in a variety of forms, be it symbols, voices or metaphors. Although I continued to be amazed each time, I was certain by now that they were real. Whether or not my mental imagery was a product of my imagination mattered little. The assurance that my spirit guide and Higher Self would be around to deliver the remedial help I needed each time was more important. Their presence was unmistakable, and undeniable. It was through their help that I gained the insightful knowledge needed to overcome the obstacles that deterred me from living at my highest potential.

I had since learned to ask, for I knew they would not intervene without my permission. I trusted that their wisdom and creativity would come up with solutions better than any human mind could ever dream of.

My mental milieu had definitely become more serene. My energy vibrations seemed to be shifting. At this time, another unbelievable opportunity seemed to "fall out of the sky". Robert, the fund manager (Chapter 3), had just made an offer to me. It was to participate in a project by his company to train people to trade in financial markets and to gauge their progress thereafter. I would be able to learn the skills from him at no cost. It was an extremely rare opportunity to learn from a successful trader! I had always wanted to invest and trade properly by myself but lacked the know-how. Now, with Robert's expertise available, I gladly accepted the offer.

This event did not strike me as coincidental. I felt it was all part of the fabric of creation and plan of the universe with a message for me about a particular facet of my life that required attention. It prompted me to understand the more profound nature of things and the wellspring of intelligence that is endlessly creating our universe.

Session 7 (Meditation): The Golden Palace and the Woodcutter's Barn

Since the meditation session on the girl in the ice land, I had been pondering over my issue of envy and jealousy, and wondered how I could overcome it. By now, most of my peers had become medical specialists and I could not help but envy their clear directions and set paths in life. I realized that such information would be impeding me more by increasing my self-doubt. Hence, I decided to probe deeper into this area of my life.

It was the morning of 31 May. I started my meditation exercise as usual. As my body relaxed and the mind went into a state of nothingness, I sought the help of my Higher Self. She appeared in my healing forest in her usual form and outfit. Next, she beckoned me to follow her.

We started walking, further and further towards the other side of the forest. After some distance, she stopped and pointed at a tree in front of us. I looked over her shoulders. There was an oval-shaped opening in the trunk of the tree, at eye level. I was not sure what she wanted. Next she told me to go near and place my face into the opening. I obeyed. Slowly, as I put my face into the opening, the scene seemed to change.

I felt like I was Alice in Wonderland. Before I could figure out what had happened, I found myself completely inside the hollow of the tree trunk. It was dark. However, I could make out a flight of black-colored steps leading downwards, and I got a feeling that I was supposed to descend the stairs.

Following my intuition, I walked down the stairs gingerly, one step at a time. In a fascinating manner, the steps started to change color as I walked, from black, to red, and to orange, followed by yellow, green, blue, indigo and violet in that order.

"These are all colors of the rainbow," I said to myself. Finally, as I reached the last step, it was gold in color. Suddenly I realized that the step was made of solid gold!

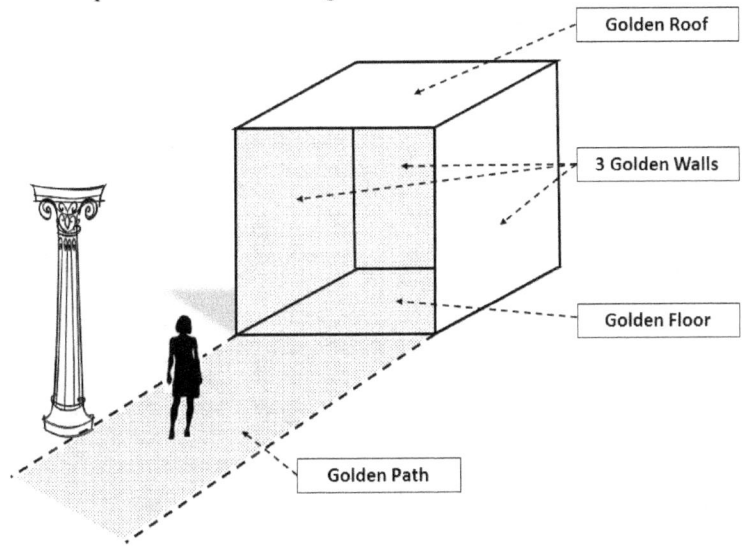

In awe, I placed both my feet on the golden step. The experience became increasingly surrealistic from this point onwards. Slowly, on its own, the step on which I was standing lengthened into a golden path. As the path emerged fully, my surroundings started to change. I saw the form of a golden palace appearing. Golden walls bordered the space, and golden pillars sprouted one by one beside the path!

As I walked down the golden path, beautiful paintings of Roman and Greek art started to adorn the walls. On walking further down, golden sculptures, again of Roman and Greek culture, occupied the space between the walls and pillars. I was overwhelmed by the richness of my surroundings. The path ended in a room bordered by three golden walls, a golden roof and a golden floor. Everything I had seen so far was made of pure solid gold.

I stepped into the room, and touched the walls. They felt smooth and cool.

Next my Higher Self appeared in the middle of the room, and we stood facing each other. She pointed at the path and as I turned my head to look back, the sculptures and paintings slowly faded out of sight. At the same time, a wall of mirror developed to enclose the golden room.

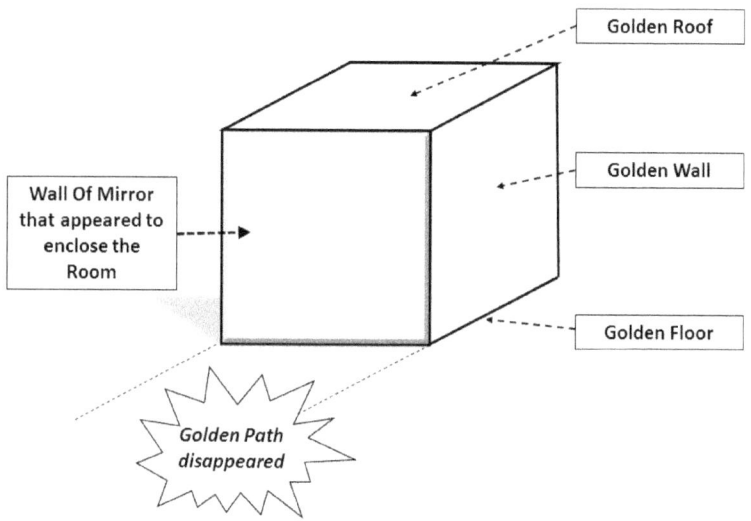

I looked at the reflection of myself and the golden room in the mirror. However, I failed to make out the reflection of my Higher Self!

I turned my head back to face my Higher Self again, and said: "I cannot comprehend. What is the meaning of all this? How is this supposed to relate to the issue of envy and jealousy?"

My Higher Self did not say anything.

The next moment, the golden walls, roof and floor transformed into large mirror-sheets.

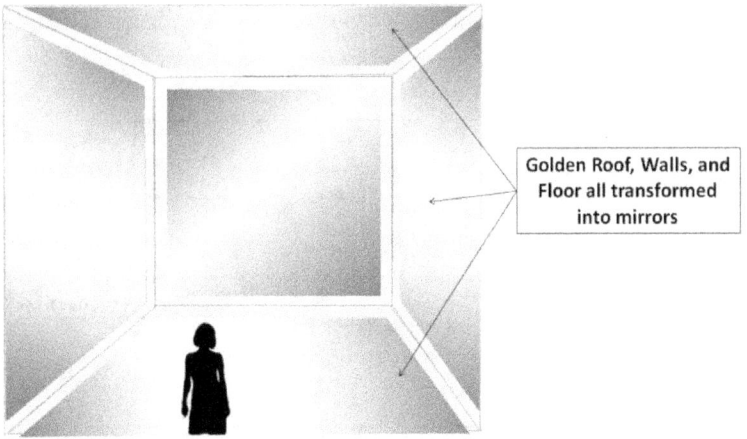

Golden Roof, Walls, and Floor all transformed into mirrors

Then these six mirrors started to move towards each other, with me in the center. I was afraid that I might be crushed, but of course that did not happen. As soon as the mirrors came close, they collapsed into me and disappeared. I was then back in the darkness again with the black flight of stairs leading upwards this time. Slowly, I ascended the stairs in deep thoughts and exited through the tree trunk again.

Outside the tree trunk, my Higher Self was waiting for me. It was a fantasy journey that I just went through, and I had yet to decipher its meaning. I turned back to look at the tree trunk, but the opening was gone and I wondered what all that meant.

Without any words, my Higher Self now signaled me to follow her deeper into the forest.

We walked a while, and reached an area of clearing. There was a barn in the middle of the clearing. The wall facing us had been removed, so we were now looking at the interior of the barn. In the middle of the barn, there was a cut tree trunk; its roots were still visible in the ground, with an axe resting on its cut surface. A fireplace was present at the other side of the barn. I realized that this was a woodcutter's barn.

A man appeared. He was the woodcutter. He seemed oblivious to our presence, and I believed it was because he could not see us. He was carrying a bundle of wood, and he dropped it on the ground. He started to chop the wood into smaller pieces. Then he threw some of the cut wood into the fireplace.

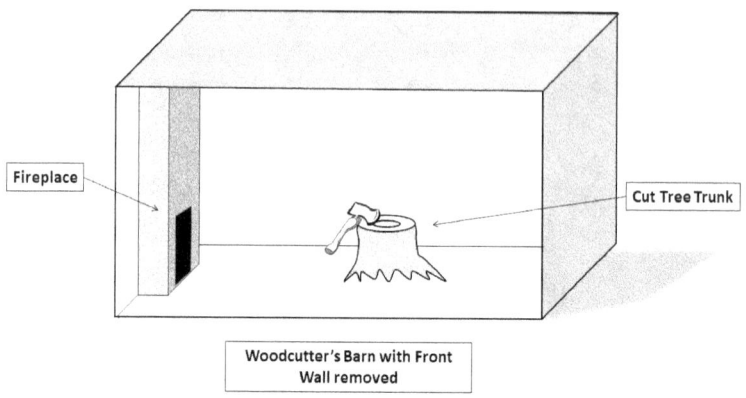

Woodcutter's Barn with Front Wall removed

Smoke rose out of the chimney. I turned to look at my Higher Self, totally confused.

"How does the golden palace and this woodcutter's barn relate to the issue of jealousy?" I repeated my question.

Again I did not hear a reply.

The scene froze and I decided to end my meditation for the day, because I was not making any headway.

Two days later, the story of the golden palace and woodcutter's barn remained vivid in my mind, but the mystery remained unsolved.

It was time for my morning meditation again. Sitting down in a relaxed position, I took a deep breath, and summoned the image of my healing forest once more. As usual, I saw the green grass, the flowing stream, the trees and the sunlight. The little bunnies had become a permanent feature in my forest, as well as the swing which was still hanging from the biggest tree that was situated next to the stream.

Lily and my Higher Self appeared promptly at my request. They were in their usual white robes. Thereafter, a cut tree trunk appeared in one corner of my forest. Next, the three of us stood around it, equidistant from each other.

The cut trunk grew into a tree, and this time, three oval-shaped openings appeared at eye level. I saw Lily and my Higher Self entering the tree trunk through the openings. I followed suit.

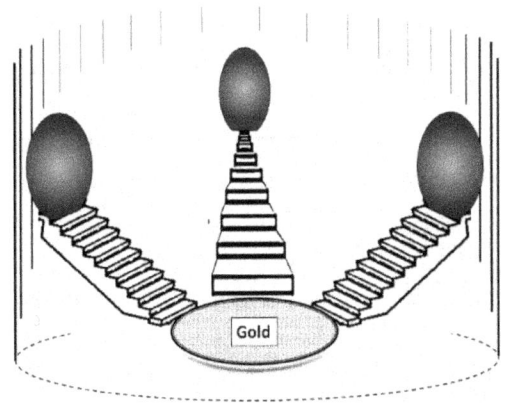

Once inside the tree trunk, darkness enveloped us. There were three flights of black stairs leading downwards, one for each of us. We started to descend on the steps. As we did so, I could see the steps converging at the bottom, where something appeared shocking.

It was a small pool of liquid gold!

Like an apparition, the pool of gold rapidly expanded and the level rose slowly towards us. I was scared! The thought of drowning in that gold did not appeal to me. Yet I could not understand why Lily and my Higher Self continued their steady descent into the pool. They seemed oblivious to the approaching danger. In a daze, I followed suit. I went deeper and deeper into the pool of gold and soon, the stuff was covering my neck. I took a deep breath, held it and prayed.

The feeling of being in the pool was funny. It was so viscous! I tried to swim but there was too much resistance. Suddenly, I sensed my Higher Self and Lily were each holding on to one of my hands, pulling me forwards. I shut my eyes tight for fear of being blinded by the gold.

After a short while, my body felt much lighter. I could tell that I was now out of the pool of gold. Lily and my Higher Self were still holding on to my hands, with Lily on my right, and my Higher Self on my left. I opened my eyes and was amazed.

I could not believe that we were flying in the sky, across the plains and seas! The wind blew across my face and I felt exhilarated!

A few moments later, we arrived at a volcano. I stepped onto the edge of the crater of the volcano, and Lily and my Higher Self let go of my hands. They told me to look into the volcano and I saw boiling lava!

Next moment, I saw the lava transforming into boiling liquid gold that was rising fast towards the mouth of the volcano. I started to panic, and reflexively used my arms to shield my body. This was when I realized I too was completely coated in gold and stiff from the earlier swim through the golden pool. There was nothing I could do as the level of the boiling liquid gold rose. As it boiled out and poured onto me, I braced myself in anticipation for the pain, but to my relief, I felt nothing. I guessed I was somehow protected by the earlier layer of gold that had coated me.

The boiling gold finally flowed down the sides of the volcano. Lily and my Higher Self motioned me to look into the crater again. I obeyed. This time, the gold was no longer there. Instead there was a clear pool of water at the bottom.

Next, the two higher beings instructed me to jump in. The pool looked so inviting that I did not hesitate. The cool water refreshed me, and for a few moments I rested my body, and relaxed myself in the pool. As I did so, I noticed the gold coating my body started to come off, and instead began coating the fishes that swam by. It was an interesting sight.

"Goldfishes!" I remarked, and laughed to myself.

Feeling light and refreshed, I emerged from the pool of water. As I did so, I looked around and saw that the scene was changing and we were surrounded by the forest again.

There was a log in the middle of a small clearing near the pool, lying horizontally on the ground. It was hollow in the middle. Lily and my Higher Self instructed me to go inside the hollow log. I hesitated, unsure what outcome the instruction would lead to, but nonetheless I did as I was told.

I carefully crawled into the hollow of the log, and it felt increasingly tight around me. I sensed a sudden change in myself. I had become the wood in the log!

In my bewilderment, I saw a man approaching. He was the woodcutter I had seen in the earlier story! He headed towards me, who was now in the form of the cut log. He started to tie several ropes around me (the log) and dragged the log back to his barn in the forest. It was the same barn from last time. Before I knew what was happening, he had proceeded to chop me (the log) up into smaller pieces for firewood!

For an agonizing moment, as he chopped, I (the chopped wood) looked towards the missing wall in his barn, and saw my Higher Self and my physical self looking at him chopping the wood! I was re-experiencing the same scene from my previous meditation session, but now from the perspective of the wood!

In that instant, I had a flash of an image of myself being the golden palace, inside every golden pillar, painting, sculpture and wall. That was why the golden walls, roof and floor had earlier transformed into mirrors and I saw myself in all of them, before they finally collapsed into me!

In a moment of truth, I heard the words: *"I am in all matter. All matter is in me."*

I opened my eyes and emerged from my meditative state. My head started to throb. Again, I was amazed at what I had experienced, but without fully appreciating how the message related to the issue of jealousy.

I rested for a moment, and closed my eyes again.

Session 8 (Meditation): One Consciousness
Very quickly I went into trance and found myself in the healing forest again. I sought Lily's help, and she appeared in front of me. This time she told me to open my right hand and show her my palm. Holding my hand, she used her right index finger to write a word on my palm. It was the Chinese character "天", meaning sky, heaven, cosmos or the universe.

This was fascinating. It was the first time that my guide was communicating with me using a Chinese language character as a metaphor.

To my surprise, the character turned dynamic! What I saw next was the character disassembling itself into components and rearranging itself consecutively into two patterns.

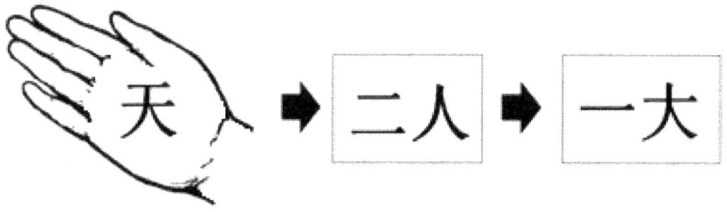

I first saw the character "天" disassembling into "二人", which literally means "two beings", a metaphor for "separation", and then the rearranging into "一大", which would translate as "one supreme".

The symbolism drove home the message immediately.

It is about the principle of the One Consciousness (or Unity) from which everything exists. Everything in the universe is a single consciousness. The universe is like the ocean and each of us is a wave in that ocean. The wave and the ocean are one and the same.

We may exist as separate individuals (二人) but we are part of a bigger unity (一大). In other words, we are all different beings and made up of separate matter, but are part of the One Divine or

Consciousness (Chapter 3). I was both the proud gold and humble wood. *I am in all matter, and all matter is in me.*

At this point, I heard Lily's voice. "Hence, you understand why there is no need for jealousy." There was an air of finality in her voice.

Enlightenment came unexpectedly again. In a blinding flash of inner light, I saw the answer to my question on jealousy. At the soul level, I saw myself in two parts. A part of my soul was localized in my body and the other part was connected to everything else. My self was inseparable from all that existed. The imagery indicated to me that what had been happening around me was but a mirror of myself and my state of individual consciousness.

It sounded profound, but having experienced a series of metaphorical narratives, I valued this insight, regardless of how esoteric the message might sound.

Therapist's Note (14): On Glyphomancy
Dr. Peter Mack

The subconscious message that Nicole received came through a process of Chinese glyphomancy (Cezi, 測字). The Chinese language is graphic in nature and the fact that most of its characters consist of more than one graphic element makes room for creativity and creation of meaning.

The segregation of the elements of a Chinese character is sometimes used to generate a new insight that differs from the original meaning of the parent word. By writing out separately the distinct parts of which a character is composed, and with these elements making new words which differ in meaning from the original, a message is obtained. This method is also used in Chinese dream analysis and divination.

Starting with an intact character "天", this was dismantled into two components "二" and "人", and these parts were then recombined into "一大", which carried a different meaning. The various combinations were then analyzed together to add to the richness of the meaning, and codified into a subtle divine message.

The reader will notice that the Chinese character elements are of two types. The first type is that of a simple indicative ideograph where each symbol bears an indexical relationship with the idea of the numerals it represents. In this case, 一 represents "one" and 二 represents "two". The second category is that of a pictograph (人) in which the pictorial symbol resembles a man. Because of the rich ideographic nature of the Chinese writing system, one is able to generate a variety of graphic puns in a way that is not possible with alphabetical languages.

I thanked Lily for her help, and I decided to ask her one final question before ending the session.

Much had transpired in the past two weeks since I reconnected with Dr. Mack. I asked Lily if these recent happenings of the past fortnight in my life were mere coincidences.

Lily picked up my left hand, and drew something on my palm again. I felt the touch and motion of her fingertip, but this time it did not feel like the scribbling of a Chinese character. I quickly opened my eyes and saw a symbol of a wheel with three radial spokes.

I slowly returned to my full conscious state again. Not knowing what this symbol meant, I subsequently searched the Internet and discovered it to be a symbol of cosmic unity. The circle is an ancient and universal symbol of unity, wholeness and infinity. Three radial spokes radiate from the center.

I was stunned! Lily was trying to tell me that what had been happening in my life recently were not mere coincidences, but a sign of cosmic unity!

Therapist's Note (15): The Law of One
Dr. Peter Mack

"Unity" is the truth and "variety" is the appearance. Each unit of the variety is identical with the One. This means our ego's covering which has been created to enclose our individuality has to be peeled off for this cosmic unity to be realized. The wise person needs to make a conscious effort to achieve this realization. This is the purpose of all our lives. So it is also that of Nicole's.

Every one of us is a unique manifestation of the Whole. Every branch is a particular outreaching of the tree. To manifest individuality, every branch must have a sensitive connection with the tree. Differentiation is not about separation. It is about being a specialized part of a more effective whole.

Cosmic unity tells that there is only one of us. We are all the same person. Your sufferings and your riches are also mine. There is no problem of jealousy as soon as one understands that envying someone is only envying oneself.

CHAPTER SEVEN

Choice and Regret

Dr. Nicole Lee

"I believe having a vision in mind, a goal, let's say, is a good thing. Unfortunately, so many of us are blinded by the greatness of our vision that paralysis and inaction sets in. What I try to do is focus on the individual steps, the moments if you will, and let them lead one to the next. The vision that eventually appears may not be exactly what you had in mind, but it will be the right one for you, because you did the work and you took the necessary action."

Charles Glassman
In: Brain Drain – the Breakthrough
That Will Change Your Life

It was wonderful to finally feel "unstuck" and have the courage to tell Dr. Mack that I was ready to move forward in my life. He raised his eyebrows and looked pleased.

Having journeyed through the adventure stories emerging from my meditative and trance states, I must admit that the insights gained were invaluable and unprecedented. I had since been able to grapple with my victim mentality and insecurity and could explain my fears in life, and envy and jealousy for other people's successes. Most of all, I was being reminded that, as a spiritual being, I was empowered to create my own reality the way I want it.

Session 9 (Regression): Love – The Magical Triangular Bowl
It was 3 June. I had arranged to update Dr. Mack of my progress in his clinic and undergo further therapy. This time I set the intention of exploring the issue of love.

As I slowly relaxed into a trance state on the couch with the help of soothing music, the theme of love surfaced in my thoughts.

Two attributes of love were pronounced – its inherent preciousness and the gentleness of the vehicle with which it was delivered. As I focused on these thoughts, I connected gently with a past event, and the image of my husband appeared.

"I recall the occasion when I ended an evening clinic session much later than expected," I began. "My husband waited patiently for more than an hour in the car so that he could send me home after my work ended. His care and concern for me just make me feel so loved."

With the thought of this love coming alive, my mind rapidly drifted into a past life scene in which I visualize myself as a pregnant lady.

"I see a big belly. I am a heavily pregnant woman, and about to deliver soon. I am wearing a white dress and white shoes, and sitting upright in a wooden chair. I live in a wooden house, and the interior looks like a Chinese building from several decades ago."

"As you are focusing on your tummy, tell me what feelings or thoughts are you having?" Dr. Mack instructed.

"I am rubbing my pregnant belly, feeling happy and excited that the baby will be arriving soon. I see a man walking up to me. I sense that he is my husband. He is not someone whom I recognize in my current life. He smiles at me, places his left hand on my shoulder, and rests his right hand on my belly. I feel his love for me, and our love for the coming baby. We feel blissful."

"What happens next?"

"He helps me up from the chair and we decide to head outside for a walk. With one of his hands supporting my waist, I walk slowly towards the open door. There is a curb at the bottom of the door, and I carefully lift my feet across it. Outside, on the left of the porch, is an old wooden rocking chair. It is bright outside and I cannot see beyond."

"Are there other people around?"

"No. I only see the two of us."

At this point the imagery came to a standstill and I had to refocus my mind.

After a momentary silence, I heard Dr. Mack's voice again.

"Tell me what happens next."

"It is a new scene now. I see myself, the pregnant woman, lying on a wooden bed in labor. Sweat is pouring down my forehead, and my face grimaces in pain. The midwife is running around, looking frantic. My husband is pacing in the room, feeling anxious. I sense something is not right. The baby does not seem to be coming out. It is a difficult labor."

"What stage of labor are you in now? Is the baby's head emerging soon?"

"No. Not yet. I am losing consciousness. The midwife has summoned help, but no one can wake me up. There is a pool of blood accumulating in the space between my thighs, staining the bed sheet. My husband is distressed, and I can sense his mounting anxiety and panic."

"What are your thoughts?"

"I am very tired."

"What happens next?"

Next, I sensed my spirit hovering above my physical body. "I have passed on," I said. "I see my pale face and motionless body lying on the blood-stained bed. The baby is still in my womb, and he too is dead. The midwife cries and shakes her head. My spirit is now floating above the body, watching the scene. I see my husband crouching over my dead body, hugging it tightly, anguished and crying inconsolably. I cannot bear to see the scene any longer. My spirit is floating away into the spirit realm."

"Are you ready to meet your guide in the spirit realm?'

"Yes ... but I do not see Lily, or my Higher Self. Instead, I see a male figure approaching me. He is wearing a long white robe, similar to what Lily and my Higher Self have been wearing. He has short black hair, and an aura of serenity around him. Instinctively, I know that he is also my spirit guide. His name just pops up in my mind – it's Thomas, but he prefers to be called Tom."

"Ask him what are you supposed to learn in this life?"

"I am still shaken from the emotions of my death. Tom is leading me somewhere and I am following him behind. We are now at a clearing. A piece of white rectangular cloth about a few meters in length appears on the ground. Then, a baby boy appears in the middle of the cloth. As I watch, the baby starts to grow into a toddler … a young boy … a teenager, and finally into a fine-looking young man. Tom tells me that he would have been my son if he hadn't died."

"What happens next?"

"I walk up to the young man and speak to him, but he does not respond. It takes me a few moments before I realize that he is an illusion. It's like a hologram projected on the white cloth. I am confused, and look at Tom for help. I ask Tom how could my baby grow up into a man when he did not even survive the childbirth?"

"What did Tom reply?"

"Tom did not say a word. He picked up a stick from the ground and drew a triangle, followed by a circle within it. Then he added a dot in the center of the circle."

"Do you understand what that means?"

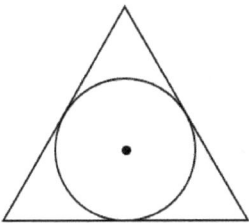

"No. I look at the image, and am wondering what it represents. Then all of a sudden, the two-dimensional image on the ground starts to transform into a three-dimensional object ... It is now a hollow cone with the dot at the cone's tip lying at the bottom on the ground."

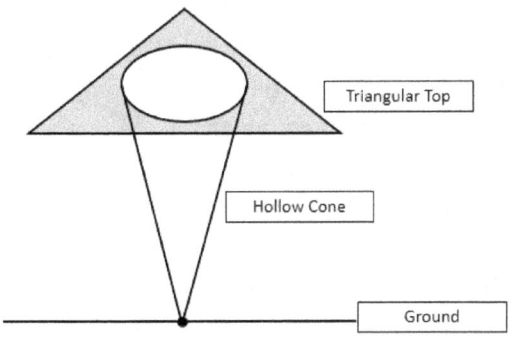

"What is this supposed to mean?"

"I don't know. The three-dimensional cone does not make any sense to me at all ... I am looking helplessly at Tom!"

The image seemed to have frozen. At this point Dr. Mack sensed my difficulty in processing the meaning of the image, and I heard him saying, "Ask Tom if there are any other messages or aspects of the story that you should know."

Upon hearing that statement, I immediately saw a change in the scene, even before I could ask.

"I see the image of a young girl and boy playing in a garden," I said. "I sense that I am the girl, now five or six years old, who will grow up to be the pregnant woman. The boy, who is seven or eight years old, is my future husband."

"Is that an earlier part of this same lifetime?"

"Yes. Since young, we like each other a lot and we spent most of our time together. While we are playing together, we are happy and carefree."

"What happens next?"

"We head back to the house. I see that the boy's parents are waiting for him. They appear well-to-do and their house is big. They smile brightly at him, and embrace him warmly. However, they frown upon noticing that I have been playing with him. I am afraid of them and quickly run away from their sight. I realize that I am one of their lowly servant girls, while the boy is the son of the owner of the household. Such is the disparity in our status, and hence we are not supposed to play together."

The scene changed again spontaneously, and at the next moment I found myself at a different stage of my life.

"I see that we have grown up and are young adults now. We love each other deeply, despite the disapproval of the boy's parents. One day, I overhear his parents telling him that they are arranging a marriage for him with the daughter of another prominent family in the town. He adamantly refuses, but there's a finality in the parents' tone. I run to my room, and cry. I know there is no chance of us ever being together, but I am not ready to let go of him. It looks like our relationship is going nowhere."

"What happens after the young man defies his parents?"

"That night, he creeps into my room, with a bag of personal belongings on his back. He reaffirms his love for me and that he will not submit to the arranged marriage. He asks me to elope with him that night. I feel my heart beating rapidly as I hurriedly pack whatever little belongings I have. We flee from the house. We eventually settle down in a remote little village and get married. I soon become pregnant with our first child. This links back to the first part where I died during pregnancy and that is how it ended. He has sacrificed everything for me but I couldn't live long enough to enjoy our time together. I have also taken his son away from him."

"Now that you have the whole story, you may like to ask Tom what is the lesson you are supposed to learn from it?"

Before I could respond, the scene transformed.

"I am now back in my healing forest, looking at Tom for help with interpretation."

"What is happening now?"

"Tom glances at the inverted cone positioned between us. The cone suddenly widens and expands to form a large bowl that is a few meters in diameter, with the triangular top at waist-level.

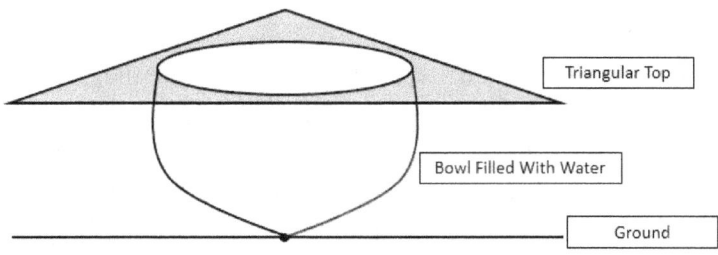

"Clear water starts filling up from the bottom of the bowl until the level reaches near the top. Tom points to the edge of the triangular top closest to me and signals me to look over the edge into the bowl of water. I follow Tom's instructions and peer over into the bowl. On the surface of the water, I see the image of the dead body of a pregnant woman lying on the blood-stained bed.

"Tom then beckons me to walk over to the next edge of the triangular top to my left, and look into the water again. This time, I see the scene of the young man asking me to elope with him. However, I am afraid and refuse to follow his plan. He is upset, and eventually marries the girl whom his parents arranged for. I stand from afar, watching the wedding ceremony, with a wrenched heart and tears in my eyes. From the images in the water, I see that he has never spoken to me or looked at me in the eyes ever since. I am being treated just as another servant in the house. The years pass and his wife bear him several children, but I know that he is never happy again. I would always watch him from afar, with my heart in pain, and hoping that if time could reverse itself, I would have eloped with him that night. Regretfully we grow old separately, and eventually die of old age."

At this point I heard the growing interest in Dr. Mack's voice. "What do you see on the third side?"

The images faded off as I lifted up my head, and glanced at Tom for permission to move on. He nodded, and I moved over to the third and last edge of the triangular top.

"I look into the water again. This time, I see myself agreeing to elope with the young man. We are running frantically through the woods away from the house. However, we are caught by the men that his father has sent to catch us. We are dragged back to the house. The father locks him away in his room. I am tied to two poles in the garden, and beaten up badly. I see his father ordering a male servant to rape me, following which I am thrown out of the house. The last scene I see in the water reflection is myself hanging from a tree outside the house in a suicidal death."

"How do you feel at this point in time?"

Tears started flowing down my cheeks. I saw myself taking a step away from the bowl, numbed from the tragedy of the last ending that I had just seen.

"The bowl has revealed the three possible endings to the story," I said. "Tom asks me if I could choose again, would I still choose the life that I have led?"

"What did you tell him?"

I paused for a moment, and answered, "Yes, I will still choose the life of the pregnant woman. I had taken the risk of eloping and led a short life with the man I loved, but the time we had together was truly happy and blissful. This short fulfilling life is worth the risk of getting caught and suffering the horrible death as shown in the third ending. It is also much more meaningful than leading a life filled with regret as reflected in the second ending. However, I feel sorry for my poor baby who has never seen the light of day, and for my husband who has to bear the grief of losing me and the baby.

"Tom then signals me to move back to the first triangular edge, and look into the bowl of water again. This time, I see my husband standing in front of my grave, grieving. His pain is heartbreaking. Next, I see him sitting alone at the table in our house. Being one of the few educated people in the remote village where we have been staying, he becomes a teacher for the village children, and also helps to read and write letters for the illiterate villagers. Even though he is lonely after I passed away, he continues to lead a simple but fulfilling life. If I were to ask my husband which ending he would choose, his answer would be the same as mine."

"So is there a parallel between this option and your situation in your present life?" Dr. Mack asked.

Upon hearing the question, I immediately saw the parallel. I did not have the courage to take risks, and as a result, I would always end up choosing the path of least resistance every time there was an important decision to make. Subsequent to that, I would continually second-guess the decision that was made, which in turn led to further regret, guilt or doubt. My life was a vicious cycle of negativity, and there seemed no way out for me until I got the message in this story.

The answer was clear. "The message is about having the courage to take risks, and not regretting the choices we make," I said. "Unlike the magic bowl of water, there is no way we can ever know what the different choices we make in life will lead to. However, there is no need to know. All we can do is to lead our current life as best as we can, treasuring whatever bliss we have, no matter how short-lived it might turn out to be. Regret does not serve any useful purpose. Nor does guilt. Every one of us has our own path to take, just like the unborn baby in the story. There is nothing to feel guilty or worry about."

The session ended at this point.

Therapist's Note (16): On Decision-Making
Dr. Peter Mack

Making a choice and sticking with it would stress some people out. That decision-making itself can be a problem because the individual is afraid of the consequences of picking a wrong choice. To some people there is a mysteriously "right" decision that needs to be identified first. He sees the act of making choices as a task to be performed rather than as an opportunity to explore possibilities.

Viewing decision-making as an opportunity to find out something new, either about oneself or another person, opens up new perspectives for growth. Unfortunately, some people perceive the opportunity as a trap, and are afraid to take the chance that they might not like the consequences. To these people they cannot go with the flow and are unable to do the thing that they do not like.

Whether a task is considered do-able or not is embedded in the individual's liking, and not in the task itself. However, such a perspective can paralyze the decision-making process. Reframing the decision positively often helps: What if making a mistake wouldn't lead to any serious consequences? Suppose no humiliation is involved in the consequences? Suppose it opens up a new, unforeseen opportunity?

CHAPTER EIGHT

Cosmic Reminders

Dr. Nicole Lee

"If we can recognize that change and uncertainty are basic principles, we can greet the future and the transformation we are undergoing with the understanding that we do not know enough to be pessimistic."

Hazel Henderson

My journal pages were fast filling up. As I turned the pages after completing my entry for my previous meditation, I thought through the spiritual messages I had received so far, and I understood that there were many more lessons in store.

Over the meditative sessions in next few evenings, I continued to receive important messages in the form of interesting stories that seemed to serve as reminders in my budding journey.

Session 10 (Meditation): A Reminder on Truth and Assumptions – The Tribal Leader and His Second Wife

It was the night of 3 June. Despite the late hour, I decided to take another excursion into my subconscious mind. I sat upright on my chair and plugged in my earphones. The soothing meditation music soon filled me with the sense of serenity that I needed for relaxation. I focused on my breathing and it was not long before I realized I was on another journey into my subconscious.

Suddenly, a fearful image appeared on my mind screen. A crouching tiger was just a few feet away from me! Its stare was so intense that a quiver of fear penetrated right through me. The animal was ready to pounce, any moment. I held my breath, my lips trembling from the imminent ending to this ferocious sight.

I realized I was now a young woman, standing alone in the woods, face to face with one of the most dangerous predators on Earth. I shivered in fear, and braced myself for the attack.

All of a sudden, an arrow flew across the trees and hit the tiger squarely on its left flank. I watched transfixed as the tiger growled in agony and collapsed onto the ground. Blood spurted out and flowed from the wound. The animal soon became motionless as the blood started to stain the soil.

A young man, dressed in tribal clothing, appeared from among the trees. Holding a dagger in his right hand, he walked up to the tiger, and stabbed it at its throat. I heard a whimper; then silence prevailed. The tiger was dead. The man proceeded to tie the animal's limbs together with a sturdy rope, and dragged the carcass across the ground.

At this point, I was still unsure where this young woman, as myself, came from. I knew that I was homeless and lost in the woods. I tried to thank the man, but no words came out from my mouth. I was still in shock at my narrow escape. He looked at me, and signaled me to follow him back to his village. I nodded my head gingerly, and followed meekly behind him.

We reached a tribal village where I saw several huts made of wood, straw and animal skins. The villagers crowded forward to welcome the man home and exclaimed at his successful hunt. I realized he was one of the young tribal leaders in the village. The villagers then turned their attention to me with a wary look on their faces. However, because of the man's status and influence, they agreed to let me stay on in the village. I had no memory of where I came from, and no inkling of where I could go next. Hence I accepted their offer gratefully.

I was given a small tent to stay in. That night, the young tribal leader came into my tent. I was thankful to him for saving my life, and had developed fond feelings for him. Hence I did not resist his sexual advances.

The next morning, I was woken up by the commotion outside. I rubbed my eyes. The man was no longer in my tent. I went out of the tent and saw a celebration. The villagers were singing, dancing, and watching a ceremony being held in the open gathering area. Curious at the event, I walked over to find out what was happening.

It turned out to be a wedding ceremony. The young tribal leader was marrying the daughter of the tribal chief! I was stunned and heartbroken by his betrayal. Next, I tried to run away from the village, but the man ordered the other villagers to bring me back. From that day onwards, I had become the unofficial second wife of the young tribal leader.

Despite his marriage to another woman and my lowly unofficial status, I still loved him, and therefore chose to stay on in the village. He was not unkind to me, but always seemed to keep a distance. I could not understand why, and wished he could reciprocate my love for him.

A few years passed, and I gave birth to his first son whom he doted on.

One day, while he was out on a hunt with the rest of the village men, his first wife barged over to my lodging with a few village women. She, unlike me, was childless. I knew she had detested my presence all along, but the feeling had turned into hatred after I gave birth to my son. I was dragged from the hut by the village women who were helping her, and they brought me to the edge of a cliff.

I cried and begged for mercy, but to no avail. Her hatred for me was too deep. My son was a few years old by now. She grabbed him and took him away from me, declaring him as her son from that day onwards. I screamed and struggled to break free of their grip, but the next thing I knew, I was pushed over the edge of the cliff!

In the next scene, I woke up, surprised that I was still alive. My eyes were blurry and my head heavy. I was not sure how long I had passed out. I surveyed my surroundings and realized I was in a fisherman's hut and there were some fishing nets hanging on the wall. I felt weak and tired.

A man appeared through the doorway, carrying a bowl. As he came near me, I looked at his face and my eyes widened in surprise. He looked exactly like my husband, the young tribal leader! He sensed my astonishment, and quickly helped me to sit up. I assumed that he was my husband, and I grabbed his arm and asked him what had happened. But the man shook his head, and told me that he was actually the younger twin brother of the tribal leader, and had been cast away from the village as a teenager. The reason was because his elder brother was afraid he would one day compete with him for the tribal headship. Since then, he had been leading a simple life as a fisherman by himself.

I was amazed by their identical appearance, but I nodded at his explanation. He told me that he had found me lying unconscious on the beach, and rescued me. I held his hands, and thanked him for saving my life.

Time passed. We fell in love, and led a quiet and blissful life together. In time I became pregnant and gave birth to a daughter. He would fish by day while my daughter and I would pick wild fruits and plants for food. He treated me very well, and I grew to love him deeply. However, I had never forgotten about my first husband (the tribal leader) and my young son. I missed them, but I knew I would never see them again. The three of them living in the tribal village were probably a much happier family now that I had left.

One day, my fisherman husband did not return from his fishing trip. It was dark, and he normally would return before nightfall. I was worried, and together with my young daughter, now four to five years old, we headed out together to look for him. We walked along the beach, and finally saw his boat floating in the shallow waters. I ran over and peered inside. There were blood stains in the hull of the boat. I started to panic. My daughter yelled and alerted me to a trail of blood on the sand leading into the forest.

I picked her up and ran towards the forest, following the blood trail. We saw him lying on the ground, with a dagger sticking out of his right flank! He was barely moving. We started to cry. I hunched over his body, and tried to lift him up. He opened his eyes feebly, and told me he was dying. "Who did this to you?" I screamed in agony. I looked at the dagger, and found its elaborate handle vaguely familiar. My husband gripped my right forearm, and said: "There is no need for revenge, just take our daughter and leave the hut. Go!"

He died. I was reeling from the shock and grief, but my survival instinct kicked in. I carried my daughter and ran back to the hut to gather our belongings, then fled into the forest.

We eventually settled down in a secluded area far away from where we lived. The years passed, and my daughter grew up into a young woman. The last scene I saw was my body on the bed. I passed away in my forties.

The image faded, and the scene changed.

I was back in my healing forest, feeling puzzled again. The story did not appear to have any parallel with my current life. While I intuitively knew that there was a message behind this story, I was unable to decipher it.

I decided to ask Tom for help and he appeared in his white robe again. His hands were clasped in front of him as he walked and he beckoned me to follow him deeper into the forest.

I followed, not knowing what to expect.

Next, I saw a white wall in the middle of the forest. It seemed out of place. There was a large rectangular mirror mounted on the wall. Tom touched the center of the mirror with his right index finger. A ripple appeared at the point of contact, and images started to appear in the mirror.

"Just like in a fairy tale!" I exclaimed to myself.

On the screen was a scene of the tribal village which I had stayed in. The tribal leader had returned from his hunt with the other men, and upon realizing that I had been murdered by his first wife, he flew into a rage and killed her! Unknown to me, he had loved me deeply, but had kept his distance for fear that his affection and attention would bring harm to me. He had been trying to protect me from the jealousy and power of his first wife. Alas! This was something I never realized, all these years!

Blinded by rage, he killed the other village women who had participated in my murder. He left the village to search for me, leaving our young son behind.

In the next image in the mirror, I saw that he had found my body, and I was barely alive. He constructed the fisherman's hut, and took care of me during the time when I was unconscious. He was actually the same person as my fisherman husband, and there was never a twin brother! I was shocked at this revelation.

He had changed his identity because he wanted a fresh start with me, as he thought that I had hated him for all these years of his cold treatment towards me, and for his wife's near-fatal assault.

Tears welled up in my eyes. "How foolish of him …" I told Tom. He did not know how much I loved him even when he was the tribal leader, and how much I missed our son. All he had to do was to ask me for forgiveness, and we could have brought our son from the village to live blissfully.

I asked Tom what happened to our son. Tom touched the center of the mirror once more with his finger, and another ripple appeared.

I saw our son, a teenager now. He was carrying a dagger in his left hand, full of anger and hatred. It turned out that he was the one who killed his own father! After his father left him behind in the tribal village, he had been ill-treated by the other villagers. He grew up in shame and had been waiting every day for his father to return and to take him away. But it never happened.

When he grew older, he started to search for his father. One day, he chanced upon the fisherman's hut that we were living in, and saw the happy life that my fisherman husband was living with me and my daughter. Filled with anger and jealousy, he waited till nightfall before he acted.

My husband was returning home alone from his fishing trip. Our son crept up behind his father, and stabbed him. Then he dragged his body into the forest. He used the same dagger that his tribal leader father had used to kill the tiger years ago.

From the images in the mirror, I saw him yelling and screaming at his father for being so selfish as to abandon him, and for all the years of maltreatment, hurt and pain he suffered as a result. His dying father begged for forgiveness, but it was too late. The son ran away, deep into the forest, and finally jumped over the cliff that I, his mother, had been thrown off years before.

What a tragedy! I shook my head; my heart was heavy from what I had just seen.

I looked at Tom, and he asked me: "Now that you have the perspectives of all the three main persons, the father, the mother and the son, what is your conclusion?"

I paused a while, and answered: "Each of them had made assumptions about how the others felt about the situation, and based on their assumptions, each individual in the story had made a fateful decision that led to this tragedy.

"The mother assumed the tribal leader did not love her. Not knowing that he had gone to such great extent to protect her, she had not looked for him after surviving the attempted murder to reclaim her son. She had assumed that the tribal leader, the first wife and the son would be living happily together now that she had left them.

"The tribal leader assumed that, as the second wife, I would hate him and not forgive him for the years of cold treatment he had given me. Hence, he decided to change his identity to start afresh with me. This was in preference to seeking my forgiveness and bringing the son back to us.

"The son, abandoned by the father, assumed that he was unloved, and became a vengeful young man. If he had approached his father and mother after locating them, he would have found out that his mother had loved and missed him all these years, and his father would have begged for his forgiveness. This would also have led to a reunion ending."

Therapist's Note (17): Narratives as Metaphors
Dr. Peter Mack

The principle of using narrative as a metaphor rests on the premise that reality is constituted by society and maintained by the members of that particular society in their stories of interaction. Thus, an emotional problem is viewed as being located within the cultural context as well as the individual's experience.

Since reality is subjective and individually constructed, there is no one "true" story. Rather each individual story is a situated, local discourse. Meaningful insight is obtained by structuring human experience into the story. Hence, the metaphoric narrative becomes a means through which a therapist can filter the patient's experiences. Under trance, the narrative forms the setting in which the therapeutic dialogue can be shaped and determines what relevant questions the patient can ask. It also explains why retelling and reliving stories has a therapeutic value.

Tom nodded his head and said: "As you can see, there were chances to make amends. But each had assumed the truth for themselves, and chosen to live by that assumption, leading to this tragic ending."

Uncertain if I had totally understood Tom, I asked if the message of the story was that we should "never assume"?

Instead of answering me, Tom bent down and plucked three blades of grass from the ground. He tied a knot in the middle of each blade, and told me to pick one.

I chose the blade in the middle. As I touched it, it transformed into a flat wooden stick with a small Chinese character at the end. I held it up for a closer look. It was the word "門" (meaning "door"). Tom plucked one more blade of grass, tied a knot in its middle and again asked me to choose from among the three blades. This time, I picked the blade on my rightmost. It too transformed into a flat wooden stick with the word "关" (meaning "close").

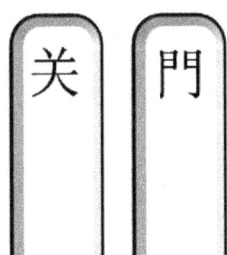

The two-word combination "关門" referred to a closed door, but I was still puzzled. Tom smiled, knowing I needed help. He picked up a branch from the ground and wrote the second character, 关 on it, but with its strokes in a backward sequence:

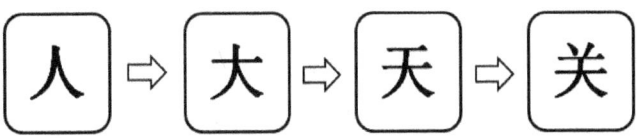

This effectively dismantled the graphic components of the word into its meaningful parts:

"人" means human, "大" means big and "天" refers to the sky or a supreme status. Metaphorically I understood this to mean that when a person is blinded by his big ego, he would close his doors (关門) to new perspectives, insights and worldviews.

I decided to probe this story further in a future session.

My meditation session ended at this point. However, I still had not answered my own question as to whether the message of the story was to "avoid making assumptions".

Session 11 (Meditation): Reminder on Mind and Openness – The Spiral Lamp

Two days passed. I was still pondering over the story of the tribal leader and his family, but had not made much headway. I decided to meditate again to seek divine help.

With my eyes closed, I drifted into a meditative state and saw my healing forest once again. This is a scene which had always helped me to become calmer and more relaxed. I waited in my forest. A few moments later, I sensed Tom's presence. This time, instead of his usual white robe, I noticed he was dressed in a light-blue robe!

I thanked him for appearing, and as usual, he seemed to know my question. He pointed to one of the larger trees in my forest and beckoned me to head over. We walked a few steps and were now standing in front of the tree.

Using his right hand, he erased a section of the rough outer bark of the tree to reveal a smooth inner layer. He then used his right index finger to draw a rectangle on the smooth bark. Next, he drew a spiral coil in the middle of the rectangle.

Tom then showed me that I could expand the coil by pulling either the inner end to form a cone, or outer end to form an inverted cone with the rectangle as the base.

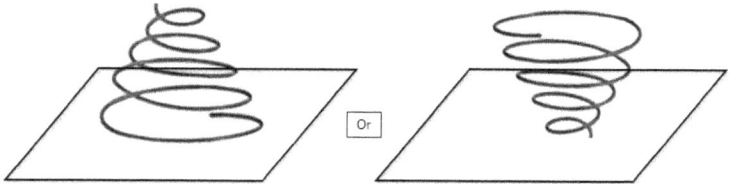

I nodded my head. He replaced the coil back to its two-dimensional form. Next, with a flick of his fingers, he removed the rectangular piece of bark and wood from the tree with the drawing of the coil still in the middle, and placed the piece of wood at my feet.

He instructed me to pull the coil from whichever end I fancied. I knelt down on the ground, and pulled the inner end of coil to form a cone. When I let go, the coil stayed in place. Suddenly, I saw the coil lighting up like a lamp, from white at the bottom of the spiral, and gradually to the different colors of the rainbow moving up the spiral. It was beautiful! The coil started to turn, faster and faster, and as it did so, all the colors blended to form white light. I was enthralled!

I heard Tom's voice asking me to look at my surroundings. I moved my eyes reluctantly from the spiraling lamp emitting white light. I suddenly realized that it was night-time in the healing forest! I looked up at the sky and twinkling stars. I looked around, and I saw fireflies dotting the forest. The air had turned cooler. I had never seen my forest at night before, and it emanated a sense of mystery and charm that mesmerized me.

I nearly forgot all about my questions until I heard Tom's voice: "What is truth?"

I refocused my attention on Tom. It was a seemingly simple but truly tough question. After a moment's hesitation, I answered, "The truth is whatever that is perceived to be true? Hmm ... I am sorry, that sounds silly. Let me try again. I guess, the truth for each person is what he or she has experienced and therefore perceives as reality?"

Tom asked me again: "So, in the tribal story, you had the privilege of seeing the happenings from the perspective of all the three main characters. Tell me, what is the truth in this case?"

I paused for a moment, collecting my thoughts. "I think in this story, from each person's experiences, he or she had assumed his/her own truth about the situation, and chosen to lead his/her life based on that perceived and assumed truth. Therefore, the truth was different for each of them. This led to misunderstandings, missed opportunities to make amends and ultimately the tragic ending. But, for the ultimate truth behind this story, I guess only the Creator will know!"

Tom smiled and presented a different question: "How do you think this spiral coil can light up?"

"I guess it absorbs the sunlight from this healing forest and therefore night falls in the forest while the lamp lights up?" I answered, shaking my head slightly. "I am not sure though."

Tom replied: "Why can't it be that night has fallen, and this is just a luminescent lamp similar in function to the fireflies?"

I shook my head more vigorously. "But night has never fallen in my forest before! I think the best way is to ask the creator of this lamp. He or she will know the truth. Oh yes ... You created the lamp from the tree. So you will know the answer!"

Tom laughed. "But remember, you are the one who decided which end of the coil to pull, and helped to create this cone-shaped lamp."

"Hmm ... that's right. So you are the main creator, and I am the sub-creator?" I replied with a chuckle, amused at the situation.

Tom smiled at me. "You see, the truth lies with the source from which all of us are created from, the One Divine as you might put it. However, from the perspective of a human, you will never know that truth because you will not be able to access it in the human form. As such, there will be gaps in the knowledge of the truth, and to live your life, you will fill up these gaps with assumptions that you make, creating the truth for your own life.

"As a human, you will make assumptions. Hence the message of the story is not to stop making assumptions, because that is impossible from the human perspective, but *to keep an open mind*. It is to know that the truth you choose for yourself has its limitations. You need to have the open mind and courage to explore the truth from other people's perspectives – that is the message.

"If the tribal leader had kept an open mind about the love of his second wife for him, he would have asked for forgiveness instead of living with the assumption that he needed to abandon his son and start afresh with a new identity. If the wife had kept an open mind about the love of her tribal husband for her, she would have looked for her husband after she survived to find out what happened and reunite with her son. If the son had kept an open mind about the love of his parents for him, he would have sought out their explanations and again, been reunited with his family. Such is the power of keeping an open mind no matter the circumstances, and giving yourself a chance to see the truth from another person's perspective."

"That explained why Tom gave me the two characters 关門 in my earlier meditation session," I thought. "When humans have big ego or are arrogant with closed minds, and assume their truth to be the Truth, heaven closes its door to further wisdom."

It was mind-blowing. The tribal story aptly illustrated this message, and Tom's explanation crystallized it all.

I thanked Tom gratefully for helping me decipher this cosmic message, and meekly asked if I could keep the lamp. He laughed and said: "This is your healing forest. Everything in here belongs to you!"

I smiled at Tom, my heart swelling with gratitude for everything he had shown and taught me. As he turned to leave, I could not suppress my curiosity and asked him why was he wearing a different-colored robe this time? I thought he always wore white!

Tom chuckled. "You assumed that I would be wearing white. That assumption is justifiable given our previous interactions. However, I pre-empted your question and am just reminding you to keep an open mind!" Our laughter rang through the forest. Tom was definitely much more humorous than what I initially assumed. Oops ... I must keep an open mind!

The spiral lamp had stopped turning by now, and it was daytime again in my healing forest. I was immensely pleased with this new addition to my forest!

Therapist's Note (18): Metaphors from the Subconscious
Dr. Peter Mack

The subconscious mind is a vast storehouse of imagery and metaphors. These are accessible at all times if the subject is relaxed and trusts the process to occur.

Metaphors have long been used in traditional healing methods and in many forms, including imagery (e.g. the spiral lamp), stories (e.g. the tribal leader) and statements generated (e.g. "this is just a luminescent lamp similar in function to the fireflies"). These complex forms are sometimes called extended metaphors, analogies or metaphorical models.

Answers from the subconscious mind are very useful for finding out more constructive ways of being. Sometimes, as in Nicole's case, it is necessary to go through several steps in order to find a response that is really useful and meaningful. In this way, the answer to one question is used as a starting point to formulate another more precise question, and so on until one feels satisfied with the final answer. Used in this manner, mental imagery plays an integrative role by bridging the conscious and the unconscious as well as the rational and the affective dimensions of one's personality.

Session 12 (Meditation): Reminder on Karma – The Female Worker and the Master

It was the evening of 7 June. I'd just had my dinner. It had been a long day. I decided to meditate as I intuitively sensed another interesting message awaiting me. I closed my eyes and started to breathe slowly, concentrating on the air flowing into my chest while trying to keep my mind free from random thoughts.

As I took a deeper breath to focus my attention, a new scene emerged.

I was sitting on a low wooden stool. I looked at my feet and they were in clogs. I realized I was a female worker in my early twenties working at a harbor, surrounded by a group of other similarly dressed female workers in dark-blue blouses and trousers. The setting seemed to be in Singapore a few decades ago. I was holding a tin container with some cooked rice and vegetables. The food did not look fresh, but it was what I had been regularly consuming for lunch.

I saw a man sitting a distance away watching the workers. He appeared well-dressed. I could not make out his facial features or expression, but I sensed that he was the boss's son, who had recently taken over the business from the father and become the new master. We were working at his construction site.

After a hurried lunch, we resumed work. I had to carry a pole on my shoulder with two baskets of soil hanging from each end of the pole, to bring the soil from one site to another for the construction of buildings at the harbor.

Suddenly, we heard a woman's cry. We crowded over to see what was happening. One of the female workers was lying on the floor, and was being beaten by the foreman. He yelled at us to get back to work, or else we would all end up like her. We scurried back to work. The ill-treatment had been occurring frequently. I glanced at our new, expressionless master, and realized that he was not a good man.

The sky turned dark. We finished for the day and headed back to our living quarters. We arrived at a large wooden house where all the female workers were staying together. We shared a common bed which consisted of a long wooden rectangular plank divided into small sleeping portions. I sat by the edge of the bed, kneading my sore muscles, tired from the long day and hard work.

To my surprise, the master appeared at the doorway. He signaled one of the young female workers from among us to follow him. She was reluctant but nonetheless obeyed. I was aware that he had been forcing those female workers whom he fancied to sleep with him. I shuddered with revulsion.

In the next scene, I saw all the female workers heading to a river to have their bath. However, the whole place was guarded by the foreman, who watched us openly. I was disgusted by the treatment we were getting, but once again I knew that there was no choice or chance of retaliation. We worked hard for our livelihood, and yet had to put up with the humiliation. I could feel the hatred towards the master surging inside me.

One night, I was summoned into his room. I tried to escape, but to no avail. My mind shut out momentarily at the violence of the next scene, but I knew he had raped me.

In the next scene, I saw myself pregnant with his child, and I was being beaten up after the master became aware of my pregnancy. I was lying in a pool of blood, weak from the beating and the miscarriage that resulted. I became motionless and the male servants who carried out the beating left me to die. Using my last ounce of strength, I crawled out of the house and tried to make it to the forest beyond the house. Suddenly, I felt a sharp pain in my back. I realized I had been stabbed by one of the male servants who came after me. I died, and the scene faded.

The last scene that I saw was that of a much older master in his study room. He was sitting at his table. He opened the first drawer at the right side of the table, took out a piece of paper, and wrote something on it. I sensed that the first four words were "生命无常", meaning that life is evanescent.

However, I noticed there were four more characters he wrote which I was not able to make out at this point in time. He then folded the paper into half, and placed it back in the drawer. He walked out of the study room, entered his bedroom and hung himself!

I was surprised at his ending, but as I was tired and could not visualize any further images, I decided to end the meditation for the evening.

I opened my eyes, and mulled over the story. It did not appear to be related to any particular life issues that I was facing, and no obvious life messages popped up at me at this juncture.

The last scene did not make sense to me either. Why would the master kill himself? He was an evil person who exploited others to his advantage, and he did not appear weak in the first part of the story. I scratched my head, and told myself I would have to discover the answers to the mysteries in a later session.

The next morning, fresh from a good night's rest, I resumed my meditation on the story again. This time, I requested Tom's help. He appeared promptly, dressed in his usual white robe. Tom brought me to a place where there was a large old bronze bell, of human height, resting on the ground. Tom motioned me to enter the bell with him. By now, I was used to exercising my "supernatural" abilities in my imagery under trance. I nodded my head, and both us "entered" the bell.

As we walked through the metallic wall of the bell and emerged from the other side, we found ourselves standing at the side of a courtyard in a house. Tom stood beside me. I realized that we were watching the scene as outsiders, invisible to people around us. There were many servants running about the courtyard, some of them carrying large bowls of water to and from the main house. Childbirth was going on in the house! Then, I saw the master of the construction company, from the earlier story, appearing from the main house. The master was anxiously giving instructions to his servants. His wife was giving birth to their second child, and he was looking forward to having his rightful heir to his business. We saw a young boy about four years old, hiding in a corner watching the proceedings. He had a huge black pigmented birthmark over the left side of his face. He was the first son, but was detested by the master because of his looks and had been hidden away from public ever since his birth. As such, the master never viewed him as the rightful heir and yearned for a "normal" son.

Suddenly, there was a commotion, and some male servants ran up to the master and reported that a female worker had escaped. At this point, I realized that this female worker referred to was myself! So, this part of the story was linked to what happened after they had beaten me up and caused my miscarriage. I heard the master ordering the servants to chase after the female worker and kill her.

A baby's cry pierced through the air. The baby was born. We saw the master anxiously rushing into the house.

Tom and I followed behind him.

The midwife was holding the baby, but her face had turned pale, and her hands were trembling. The master looked at the baby, and instantly his face contorted into rage. He screamed in agony and grabbed the baby from the midwife, holding it above his head, and nearly smashed the baby onto the ground had the midwife not caught the baby in time.

I peered over at the baby. He had a similar black pigmented patch over his left face, just like the elder son! The master collapsed onto the chair, in shock and disbelief. He ordered the midwife to get the "monster" out of his sight and said he never wanted to see him again.

The midwife hurriedly left the house. Tom and I followed behind her. We saw that she could not bear to kill the boy but she knew no one would dare to keep him. She wrapped the baby in a white blanket, placed him in a basket and floated the basket down the river which led into the woods. The basket finally wedged between some rocks, and the boy was rescued by an old woodcutter who lived alone; he decided to raise him as his own son. The boy grew up to be a fine, intelligent young man. The pigmentation on his face faded over the years, and only a faint mark remained on his forehead.

The old woodcutter grew ill, and before he died, he told the young man to head into the city and look for a person who owed him a favor from many years ago. He passed a piece of paper to the young man, and said that the person would give him a job upon seeing the paper. He told the young man that he was too intelligent and talented to continue leading his life as a woodcutter.

After the old woodcutter died, the young man followed his wishes and sought out the person in the city. It turned out that this person was now the owner of one of the largest construction companies in town, and was the main rival to his father's company. He was given a job, and over the years proved his worth with his hard work and intelligence. He eventually rose in rank to become one of the stakeholders of that company.

In the meantime, the master, who was saddened over the lack of a rightful heir, became depressed, and his company declined over the years. It was eventually acquired by the company that the young man now owned part of.

On the day of signing the acquisition contract, the master saw the young man for the first time. He recognized that this was the boy, his son, whom he'd ordered to be killed years ago, yet who in turn grew up to be the heir he had yearned for all his life.

That night, he entered into his study, and wrote down these eight Chinese characters: "生命无常", meaning life is evanescent, and "因果报应", meaning karma or cause-and-effect, before hanging himself in his bedroom. This was part of the last scene that I saw in my earlier meditation the evening before. I remembered I did not manage to the see the last four characters during that session.

There still seemed to be a missing part in the story. So I asked Tom about the significance of the role of the female worker in this story. Tom revealed to me that after the female worker was raped by the master, she went to look for the midwife and bribed her to poison the master's wife so the baby would be born deformed! The midwife could not bear to kill the baby because she was the one responsible for his plight.

Tom and I exited the bell. I understood now that this story was about cause-and-effect, also known as karma. The master wrote the last eight characters before his death because, to him, his wealth and status were impermanent, and his evil deeds of raping his workers and killing the children born by the women he raped led to his downfall by the very son he tried to kill. On the other hand, the revengeful act by the female worker to harm an unborn child also planted the seed for her own fateful ending.

Tom said: *"What you do unto others, others do unto you."*

He then picked up a branch from the ground, and proceeded to strike the bell three times. I covered my ears at the loud chiming and asked Tom, "What did that mean?" Tom chuckled and replied: "Nothing, just to drum the message into your head!" I laughed.

Therapist's Note (19): On Karma
Dr. Peter Mack

The word *karma* is derived from a root word which means to act, to make or to do. Accordingly, any action, be it mental or physical, is called karma, but it is to be noted that the word encompasses both the cause and the effect of the action and includes both sacred and secular deeds. The word is also sometimes understood as fate, referring to certain consequences of acts in a previous incarnation.

In general, the concept can be expressed as "good deeds bear good fruits, and evil deeds bear bad results". There is theoretically no escape from the results of karma, but the results of a person's deeds may not necessarily appear in his present life. In this regard karma presupposes rebirth, and in order to reap the results of one's deeds, one has to be born again. Thus, karma regulates not only the past and present but also the future.

I ended my meditation session, and thought for a long time about the story I had just experienced. Many a time in the physical world, life appears unfair as we see unkind people leading a seemingly good and rosy life, while other more deserving humans struggle with daily survival. Yet, at the divine level, nothing can be unfair, and the mechanism to balance out the unfairness is through karma. As I moved on ahead in my newfound lease of life, I would remind myself of the cause-and-effect of everything I do, because there is certainly more to our existence than what our five physical senses can perceive.

CHAPTER NINE

Inner Healing

Dr. Nicole Lee

"We are healed of a suffering only by experiencing it to the full."

Marcel Proust

It was late night on 9 June. I was still intrigued by the cosmic reminders I had received during my meditations in the past few days, and I was determined to continue exploring.

Session 13 (Meditation): The Cave and the Stone
I closed my eyes, and an image of my healing forest appeared at once. The swing which appeared during my earlier meditation session was now a permanent feature in my forest. I walked over to swing on it, enjoying the motion of the swing and the wind blowing against my body. Having an activity to perform while I was in my healing forest helped me to keep my random thoughts at bay.

All of a sudden, a dwarf appeared from the other side of the forest! I had never seen him before, and was taken aback at his entry to the scene. He looked rather irritable and the word "Grumpy" came into my mind. He looked just like Grumpy in *Snow White and the Seven Dwarfs*, and I could not help but chuckle to myself. That seemed to irritate him further, and to appease him, I addressed him as "Sir" in front of his name. That seemed to work.

Sir Grumpy motioned me to get off the swing and follow him. I was curious as to what was in store and followed promptly. We walked a short distance and reached the entrance of a large stone cave. We entered the stone cave. I looked around, and saw only stone walls with nothing special. Next, he pointed to a small rounded stone on the ground.

Sir Grumpy did not like to speak, and instead motioned me to pick the stone up. I walked over to where the stone was lying, picked it up with my left hand, and when I turned it over, I noticed green moss at the area where the stone was in contact with the ground. Similarly, there was a layer of green moss on the area of the ground on which the stone had been resting.

Suddenly, leaves started to sprout from the green moss on the ground! Soon a huge stalk appeared, and it grew rapidly upwards through the ceiling of the cave. "This looks like the fairy tale, *Jack and the Beanstalk*!" I exclaimed to myself.

Sir Grumpy then pointed to the side of the stalk facing away from me. I walked over to take a look. To my horror, this half of the stalk was completely black in color! Perplexed, I peered again to take a closer look, and realized that the black color was composed of a tight mass of ants!

I recoiled from the stalk in fright, and took a glance at Sir Grumpy. He did not heed my discomfort, and instead instructed me to place my right hand on the mass of ants! I shook my head furiously and refused. However, he became even grumpier and insisted I obey his instructions.

I hesitated, but eventually obeyed. Holding my breath, I cautiously placed my right palm over the mass of ants, expecting myself to be bitten or run over by them. To my astonishment, they all disappeared at my touch! Next moment, the stalk started to turn into gold! I had the Midas touch!

I shouted out in amazement! This story was turning out to resemble a condensed version of the fairy tales! I proceeded to touch the walls of the cave with my right palm, and soon the whole cave had turned into gold!

Sir Grumpy and I stood in the middle of the cave looking at the golden sight. All of a sudden, the walls of the golden cave collapsed onto us! I involuntarily put up my hands to shield myself, but Sir Grumpy just remained where he was, seemingly oblivious to the impending danger. Just before being crushed, the pieces of golden walls disappeared into thin air, and we were back at the stone cave once again.

I shifted my visual attention back to the small rounded rock which was back on the ground. There was no sign of any beanstalk or ants this time. Sir Grumpy instructed me to pick up the stone again. Once again, there was green moss at the bottom area of the stone and on the ground. In the next instant, the beanstalk sprouted up again. This was a repeat of what I had just experienced! I placed my right palm on the ants, and once more, everything turned to gold, and then collapsed onto us again. Then the stone cave reappeared, with the small rounded stone on the ground yet again.

This was Groundhog Day,[8] I remarked to myself. After several rounds of the same scenario, I grew restless and finally decided to do something different.

I took another look at the mass of black ants. Now Sir Grumpy had stopped giving me instructions, seeing that I had gotten the gist of what was happening. This time, instead of using my right hand, I instinctively held up the small rounded stone in my left hand. I looked at the area of green moss at the bottom surface of the stone, and brought this area to touch the ants instead, not knowing what might happen.

This time, instead of turning into gold, all the ants disappeared, and the stalk turned green like the other side! All of a sudden, flowers, leaves, and trees started sprouting out from the ground of the cave! I looked in amazement at the flourishing greenery, and realized that the cave was transforming into my healing forest! At the same time the giant beanstalk had transformed into the largest tree in my forest, from which my swing was now hanging (Session 6).

"So, this is the origin of my healing forest!" The thought jumped into my mind.

I could hardly contain my exhilaration. For once, Sir Grumpy's lips tilted slightly upwards, barely resembling a smile, and he seemed pleased with me. He waved his arms, and a stream appeared across the forest floor. It was his gift to me for solving the mystery.

As he left, I heard the words echo through my forest: *"When the created contacts the creator, healing begins."*

I was dumbfounded for a moment, but soon the meaning becomes clear. When the beanstalk (representing the *created*) contacted the stone (representing the *creator*), it led to the origin of my *healing* forest. When we, as individual souls, come into

---

[8] *Groundhog Day* is the name of a 1993 American fantasy comedy. It is about a TV weatherman who finds himself in a time loop, repeating the same day again and again, and after several suicide attempts begins to re-examine his life and priorities.

contact with our Creator, the One Divine, inner healing begins. Wasn't this what had been happening to me?

Therapist's Note (20): On Healing and Meaning
Dr. Peter Mack

To heal means "to make sound or whole" and originates from the root, *haelan*, the state of being *hal*, or whole. *Hal* is also the root of "holy", which means "spiritually pure".

Although Medicine is traditionally considered a healing profession, its modern focus is on diagnosis, treatment and prevention. Hence its primary purpose has somewhat shifted from care to cure. Hence, healing, in the holistic sense, is rarely talked about because it is considered as beyond Medicine's orthodoxy and more befitting of complementary and alternative care.

Healing is currently regarded as a process of bringing together different aspects of the individual's self, or body-mind-spirit, at deeper levels of inner knowing so that it leads to integration and balance. It is understood that all aspects of the body-mind-spirit are of equal importance and value. Inherent in the concept is the idea of "being whole". To be whole as a person is to be whole among others and involves all four dimensions of physical, mental, emotional and spiritual aspects of human experience.

The sense of wholeness is difficult to define. It is better experienced in connection with others. An individual may feel that he is suffering because he is not the person he has known himself to be. The feeling may be associated with a sense of isolation and loss in capacity when he cannot do the things he used to do. Healing can proceed independently of any associated illness or physical impairment. In fact illness can facilitate a connection, and lead to a re-interpretation of life, within the life narrative of the individual. An illness may be regarded as a "disease of meaning" in the sense that it represents various aspects of an individual's life in which these aspects can serve as a source of growth, understanding and opportunity for greater awareness. Ultimately the process reflects the meaning attributed to his illness, life-stressors and worldviews. With this depth of meaning, a disease can be perceived as a catalyst for the individual to grow and heal. It is also a link between the individual's self-perception and meaning to the problem.

I cherished the gift of my healing forest. This little story of the "The Cave and the Stone" served as a reminder for me that from now on, I should learn to trust my intuition to guide me in making choices and decisions that would enhance my healing. This would bring me closer to my spiritual self and the Creator.

The next morning I woke up to document the story of the cave and the stone that I experienced. As I flipped through the pages of my journal, I could hardly believe the surge of messages and stories that had come into my mind ever since I commenced my healing journey.

Within the span of three weeks, I had gained invaluable insights into the issues that had enslaved me for more than ten years. I felt as if this spiritual boost was to make up for all the lost time I had used in negating and neglecting my spiritual self, which had led to my over-emphasis on the material values typified by the physical world.

Session 14 (Meditation): Three Dynamic Tarot Cards
It was the evening of 10 June as I commenced my meditation session again. As usual, I decided to call up the image of my healing forest and stayed relaxed within it. I mentally turned on my spiral lamp (from Session 11), and as it spun, night fell in my healing forest. I gazed at the twinkling stars as I oscillated on my swing. It felt truly tranquil!

Sir Grumpy suddenly emerged from the trees again, and urged me to follow him. I was reluctant to interrupt my peaceful state, but nonetheless I got off the swing and followed. As we walked deeper into the forest, I noticed that the two little bunnies were tagging along. How adorable! I smiled. Little did I realize that they too had a role to play as the story progressed.

We walked a short distance and reached a small cottage in the middle of the forest. Judging by the size of the building and the height of the entrance door, low-sited windows and the straw roof, I knew that it belonged to Sir Grumpy. Carefully, I bent my head over to get through the door and enter the cottage.

Once inside, it was another fairy tale scene. In the middle of the room, there was a giant mushroom with a flattened top that was being used as a table. On top of the mushroom table was a set of Tarot cards laid out face down neatly in a row. Sir Grumpy sat down on one side of the table and signaled me to sit down opposite him.

He pointed to the deck of cards and indicated to me to pick up three cards randomly. I was largely unfamiliar with the Tarot. As far as I could recall, my previous exposure to the Tarot amounted to only a few curious glances at the cards displayed in a funfair booth and in movies.

With mixed feelings, I ran my fingers from left to right over the row of cards. Gently, I paused on top of one card and slid it out of the row. Next, I selected two more cards similarly, and arranged them in a row.

Sir Grumpy waved his hands and the rest of the unchosen cards disappeared, leaving the three cards on the table.

I flipped over the first card on my left. It showed a man standing upright, holding a sword with both his hands (Page of Swords). I next flipped over the middle card. It revealed a woman holding a vessel resembling a bowl containing water in front of her (Queen of Cups). As my Tarot knowledge was minimal, I did not know the names of these two cards nor their underlying meanings. Finally, I flipped over the last card on my right. It was the Devil card, and it was the one and only card in the Tarot deck that I recognized.

Sir Grumpy waved his hand again and a clear bowl of water appeared on the table between us. By now, I was used to his magical hands. He picked up the first card with the man holding a sword and placed it into the bowl of water. The card dissolved in the water and left behind the image of the man with the sword on the surface of the water. The man started to move and swing his sword downwards before regaining his original posture. This motion was repeated again and again.

Next, Sir Grumpy placed the second card with the woman holding the vessel in the water, next to the moving man. The card dissolved too, and the woman started moving also. She knelt down on one knee, and simultaneously lifted up the vessel to her right. As she did so, the sword that was held by the moving man swung down on the vessel, halving it and causing water to spill vertically downwards from the split vessel. The image of the man bisecting the vessel as the woman was lifting it up repeated itself over and over again. Frankly, I had no clue what was going on!

Finally, Sir Grumpy placed the Devil card in the water, above the images of the moving man and woman. The card also dissolved, and the image of the Devil remained, watching over the repeating scene below him.

Therapist's Note (21): On the Tarot
Dr. Peter Mack

The Tarot is a pack of seventy-eight cards that have been used in Europe since the mid-fifteenth century. Initially used for games, it has since evolved into a tool for divination and mapping of mental and spiritual pathways, because of the rich symbolism of its images.

The pack has two parts: (i) twenty-two cards of the Major Arcana which is filled with wisdom from multiple cultures and esoteric traditions and meanings that illustrate the structure of human consciousness; (ii) fifty-six cards of the Minor Arcana which consists of four suits – Swords, Wands, Cups and

> Pentacles, each of which corresponds to a different facet of day-to-day life. Each suit in the Minor Arcana consists of fourteen cards, including ten numbered cards (Ace through Ten) which reflect everyday life situations and four Court cards (Page, Knight, Queen, King) which reflect personality types.
> The Devil card belongs to the Major Arcana and carries the symbolic meanings of bondage, addiction and materialism.

In the next instant, not knowing what came over me, I lifted my right hand and moved it towards the bowl on the table. It was as if I was acting reflexively to the imagery before me. I used my index finger to flick the images of the man and woman apart. Then, I moved the Devil down between the two of them. This time, as the man's sword swung over, it slashed the Devil, whose blood began flowing into the vessel that the woman was carrying.

Suddenly, the bowl on the table turned blood red! I blinked, and in the next moment, everything disappeared!

I was now back in the middle of the unfamiliar forest, and the trees around me started to spin faster and faster! I felt dizzy and terrified, wondering whether I had done something wrong.

When the spinning finally stopped, I realized I was lost and did not know my way back to my healing forest. Thankfully, the two little bunnies that had followed us seemed to know the way. I followed their lead, and managed to reach my own healing forest shortly.

I sat on the floor of my healing forest, dazed at what had just happened. Sir Grumpy appeared and sat down opposite me. He then transformed into the Devil character himself. I noticed that he was not pleased, but I could not understand why or what he was hinting at. After a short while, the Devil character transformed back to Sir Grumpy's original appearance, and he left my healing forest.

I felt confused, and for some reason there was a sense of unease. I opened my eyes and awakened from my meditation.

That night, I had a fitful sleep. I fell asleep only to awake repeatedly. I experienced bizarre dreams. I woke up the next morning, still feeling odd about the imagery I had encountered the night before and my incomprehensible action in flicking the images of the Devil between the man and woman. I kept seeing the images in my head.

All of a sudden, an enlightening thought dawned on me!

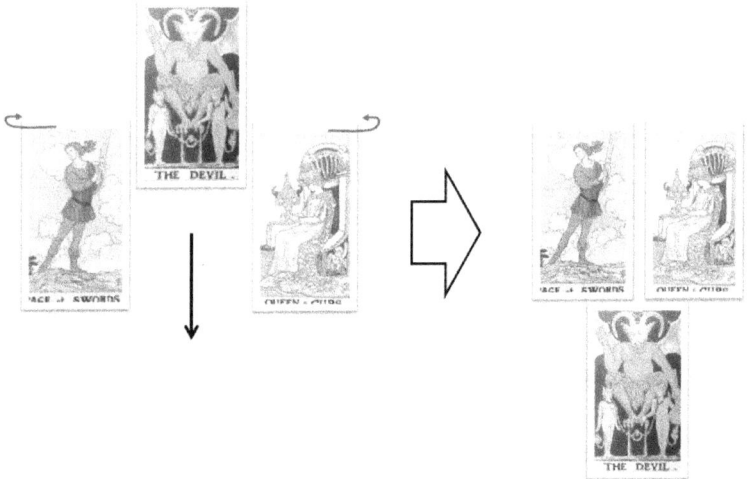

I realized that I should have flicked the image of the Devil all the way downwards so that he stayed below the man and woman, rather than in between them! Once again, I did not know where this thought came from, but the feeling of being right was hitting me strongly.

I quickly positioned myself and slid into a meditative state. I connected with Sir Grumpy again and visualized myself following him to his cottage once more, back to the site of the table with the Tarot cards. This time, I flicked the images of the man and woman apart, and as the man lifted his sword to repeat the swinging motion, I rapidly moved the image of the Devil downwards. Then I flicked the images of the man and woman back next to each other. The Devil was therefore now below the man and the woman. As the man's sword halved the woman's vessel, water from the vessel flowed onto the Devil, and as it happened, the Devil lost his horns and changed into a man-like character!

"I did it!" I said to myself.

At the same time, I stared in awe at the transformation. In the next instant, everything started to disappear again. However, instead of finding myself lost in the unfamiliar forest, I was now looking at a beautiful waterfall! Sir Grumpy was standing next to me, and I could sense that he was immensely pleased.

Somehow, with the slight change in the position of the Devil, I had managed to "solve" his riddle, even though I still did not understand the significance of the dynamics thus far. However, I decided to just bask in the magnificent beauty of the waterfall before me as I realized this was Sir Grumpy's gift to me for solving the riddle. He was definitely much more generous than he appeared!

After a while, I realized that the waterfall was connected by a short path to my healing forest. It looked like I now possessed a new additional feature to my healing place.

After emerging from my meditation, I was so intrigued that Tarot imagery had appeared in my meditative state with this inordinate amount of detail that I decided to surf the Internet. Besides the Devil card which I had seen in the movies before, I had no idea what the other cards in the Tarot deck looked like. Hence, imagine my surprise when the images of the lady with the vessel of water and man with a sword turned up in my Google-search as the Queen of Cups and Page of Swords respectively! Moreover, what did their combined motions signify? What did the resulting transformation of the Devil into a man-like figure mean? Nothing made sense to me at this point. I was puzzled.

For the next two days I researched into the meaning of the Tarot cards but did not make any headway. The curiosity was building up in me. I finally relented and decided that I needed to seek Sir Grumpy's help once more.

This time, as I entered into the meditative state, I saw myself at the waterfall, admiring the sounds of the gushing water, and the brilliance of the sunlight as it refracted through the water. I sat down on the forest floor next to the waterfall and waited for Sir Grumpy. He appeared and sat down opposite me. Like my other spirit guides, he seemed to know my question without asking. He pointed his fingers at the two little bunnies beside us, and they transformed into the Page of Swords and the Queen of Cups instantly.

The Page started to swing his sword repeatedly, just like the image in the bowl of water. I realized Sir Grumpy wanted me to look at the repeating motion. As the sword moved again and again, its motion seemed to represent a circle!

Similarly, as the Queen knelt down and lifted the vessel up to her right repeatedly, the movement of the vessel being lifted up towards the right seemed to represent an arc! As the water flowed down from the halved vessel, the motion of the water seemed to represent a vertical line.

Sir Grumpy then transformed a rock into the image of the Devil. Finally, as the water dripped down and contacted the Devil, it transformed into a man-like creature.

Alas, the key to the meaning seemed to reside in the circle, the arc and the vertical line. Whatever their meaning, the outcome of their interaction seemed to be leading to transformational change.

I awakened from my meditation, and hastily Googled about the symbolic meanings behind the circle, the arc and the vertical line. The following information was uncovered.

The circle is the symbol for completeness and the soul, whereas the arc represents ascension or striving. The vertical axis symbolizes the connection between the earth and the spiritual realm. Combining all these symbols and the image of transformation, I gathered that the cosmic message was that if I strive (arc) towards completeness and my soul (circle), then there will be a path between the earth and the spiritual realm (vertical line). This path would in turn lead me to my transformation (Devil changing into a man).

This explanation felt right, but I sensed there was more beyond what my rudimentary knowledge of Tarot symbolism could unravel. I decided it was time to seek Dr. Mack's help!

CHAPTER TEN

Tarot Imagery and Healing

Dr. Peter Mack

"The future is an imaginary solution to the problem of the present and the Tarot offers imaginary solutions to the problem of our lives. It does so by having us swerving away from our remorse about the past and our anxiety about the future, into the increasingly rare experience of the present. The Tarot is one of the fastest ways we have to get where we were not going."

Enrique Enriquez

Nicole's question about Tarot symbolism came as a complete surprise. In the first place, this esoteric knowledge area was something that I had been keeping private for many years. However, as she was at the stage where the meaning of the Tarot was critical for her healing, it became imperative for me to explain the Tarot symbolism in detail.

While many people know of the Tarot as a divinatory tool, few are aware of the multiple layers of spiritual wisdom embedded in its system of images. The Tarot is steeped in allegory. All its images revolve around the story-telling of human life, experiences and situations. The pictures within represent the gamut of emotions and circumstances that we experience in our lives and are a mirror reflection of all our joys, struggles, fears, passion and growth. Its imagery is designed to project the possibilities of how one may influence a situation in life. Hence a lot can be learned about ourselves from reading a simple Tarot spread.

The Tarot deck contains seventy-eight cards and has two component parts: twenty-two cards of the Major Arcana[9] and fifty-six cards of the Minor Arcana, which in turn is divided into four suits: *Wands, Swords, Cups* and *Pentacles*. The four suits represent the mundane activities of our day-to-day life. The Wands stand for action, motion, optimism, adventure and struggle. Swords stand for mental activity, freedom, intellect, conflicts, anger or disturbed emotions. Cups stand for feelings, quiet reflection, experience, love, friendship and joy. Finally, the Pentacles stand for materialism, work, money, routine activities.

A Journey through Life (Major Arcana)
The twenty-two cards of the Major Arcana use archetypes in its image system and represent a rich philosophical meaning of our existence. Arranged in sequence, they constitute a pictorial representation of the stages and experience of one's journey through life, from differentiation to integration. The twenty-two cards represent a path to spiritual self-awareness and depict the various milestones in one's life as one searches for meaning. Each Major Arcana card is numbered, following a sequence of archetypal life stages from the beginning (The Fool, Card 0) to the end (The World, Card XXI). Each Major Arcana card represents a stage in the Fool's journey, an experience that an individual must connect with to realize his wholeness.

The whole life journey can be viewed as a journey through cycles. The issues affecting oneself will reverberate through the cycle and impact on the journey through all subsequent cycles. The journey is really about the emergence of the ego and letting go of it when one incarnates into this world. In the process, the individual learns lessons that are useful to the overall journey of the soul.

---

[9] Arcanum means secret knowledge.

The journey starts with the undifferentiated unity of the first card, the Fool (Card 0) towards the direction of differentiated union, the World (Card XXI), which is the card of completion. The Fool stands for each of us as we begin our journey through life. We are a simple soul with innocent faith to undertake a journey that involves hazard and pain. The divine spirit (fool) is embedded in the physical body and the journey makes a person more differentiated as he identifies things, forms paradigms and experiences various events through the journey. Sometimes he moves on blindly, and at other times, consciously. Moments of crisis can lead to moments of spontaneous awakening. During his moments of awakening he realizes that he is on his way home and moving towards a differentiated state. The challenge of the life journey is the challenge of knowing oneself.

THE FOOL.

As the individual (Fool) sets out, he encounters the Magician (Card I), which represents his conscious awareness, followed by the High Priestess (Card II), which represents his mysterious unconsciousness, or intuition. The Magician is the force that allows him to impact the world through a concentration of will and power. The High Priestess, on the other hand, provides the fertile ground on which he realizes his creative potential and intuitive power.

As the individual grows, he comes to know his mother figure or nurturer as represented by the Empress (Card III), who symbolizes the world of nature, sensation and abundance. Next he encounters his father figure as represented by the Emperor (Card IV), who symbolizes structure and authority.

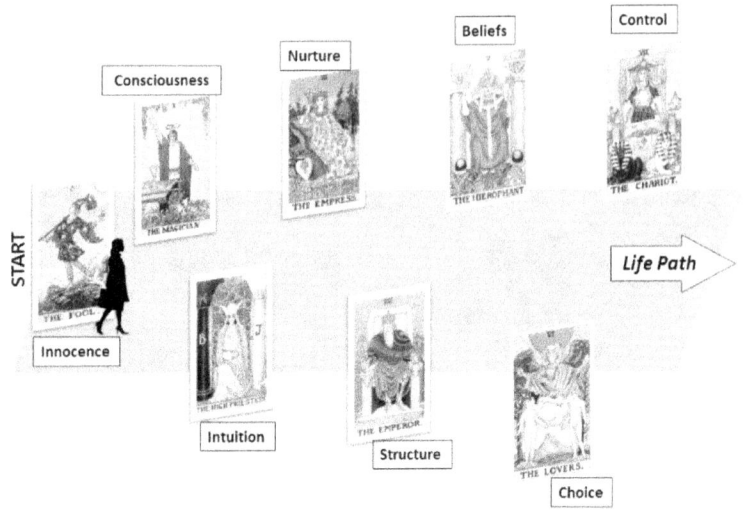

Then he discovers order and patterns in the world. Eventually, when he ventures out of his home into the wider world, he is exposed to the beliefs and traditions of his culture as represented by the Hierophant (Card V). At this stage he begins his formal education and starts to identify himself with particular ways of life as he conforms to the social structure around him.

As the individual grows, he starts to yearn for companionship and sexual union with another person. The Lovers (Card VI) tells him to make good and balanced choices and not to let his emotions get the better of him. By this time, he is developing a certain amount of self-control and a sense of who he is. The Chariot (Card VII) represents his ego and illustrates his ability to see both sides of an issue to make better decisions. He recognizes his own strength to maintain order in the midst of chaos. As time passes he encounters challenges and he needs to draw on his inner strength to keep going as represented by Strength (Card VIII). He is forced to learn to control his instincts and impulses and master his self-control.

At a certain point in his life he begins to ask the question "Why?" as he searches within himself for answers. The Hermit

(Card IX) represents a turning inward and a questioning of all he has learned to ensure that his beliefs reflect his learning. He needs quiet moments and solitude to search for his purpose of life. After a period of introspection, he sees how things fall into place and finds a sense of inner peace. The Wheel of Fortune (Card X) symbolizes how the universe works in harmony. He has grasped some of the answers he has been searching for and sees how his destiny plays out as he approaches a turning point in his life.

After some soul-searching he sees himself as part of a bigger plan. At this point he looks back at his journey so far and takes responsibility for his past actions. The Justice (Card XI) teaches him about truth and fairness and that he reaps the benefits of what he sows. He must make amends where necessary, and move on.

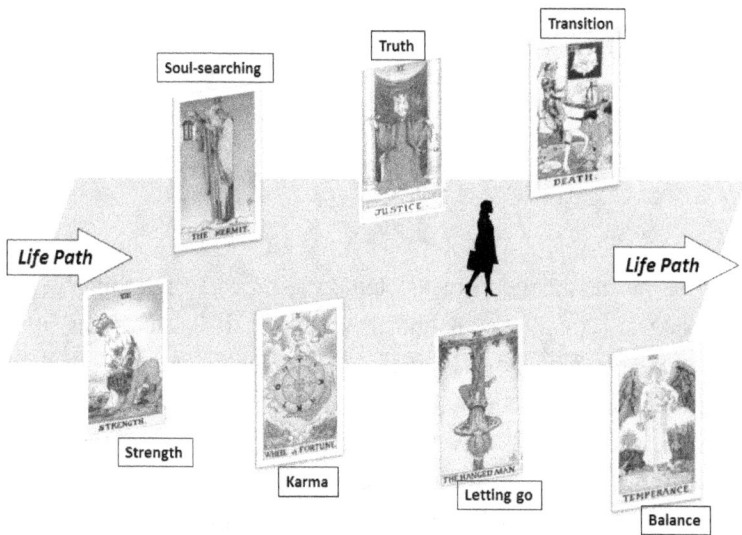

Next the individual is determined to realize his dreams but finds that life is tougher than he thinks. The Hanged Man (Card XII) teaches him the power of letting go. With this, he is able to see the world through a different perspective and the importance of sacrifice. He realizes that a major change is now necessary. The Death (Card XIII) reflects a transition and an important moment of transformation in his life. He knows that he needs to abandon his old self in order to learn something new. He has met death, the ultimate change and has learned to see the world from a new perspective with equanimity. After experiencing emotional extremes and challenges on his journey so far, he now realizes that balance is the key. Temperance (Card XIV) tells him the importance of adapting to changes in circumstances while maintaining his sense of self.

Once he has learned not to blame the universe for things that go wrong, he starts to confront his shadow self that controls him in subtle ways. The Devil (Card XV) represents bondage, or what can happen if he lets his life goes out of balance. At some level, the Devil card represents his ignorance and the hopelessness residing in him. He needs to undergo a sudden and catastrophic change to release himself from his inner prison. The Tower (Card XVI) stands for destruction and provides him with the needed opportunity. The destruction takes away what is obsolete and brings change and truth with it. He now realizes the truth that has caused the foundation, on which he has placed his hopes, to crumble.

When the individual is at the very bottom and has lost all his belongings in the destruction, the Star (Card XVII) provides hope, guidance and optimism. The Star shows him a new path to enlightenment. At this point in the journey, he is susceptible to fantasy and a false picture of the truth. The light of the Moon (Card XVIII) can be misleading because it shows things under a deceptive light. He must learn to move among illusion and hidden influences. Next the Sun (Card XIX) shines into his hidden places to dispel his confusion and fear. He starts to understand the goodness in the world. Warm, vital forces reinvigorate his journey and he feels close to his achievement. He has finally learned who he is and Judgment (Card XX) calls him to come to an even deeper state of spiritual realization through rebirth. He has learned to forgive himself and others and discovered his true purpose. With a more complete understanding of himself and his place in the world, he has now come a full circle. The World (Card XXI) symbolizes his achievement, attainment of his goal and the ending of a difficult but propitious travel. By then, he is no longer the innocent person he used to be.

The World (Card XXI) has a special significance for Nicole's journey. It is the gateway for her new beginnings after charting her path and surmounting her obstacles. The androgynous figure and the circle in the card symbolize a union of the conscious with the unconscious, or the body and the mind. All that remains is her union with the One Divine, in whatever form it comes. The lessons learned are being put to use, and her accomplished tasks are bringing fruit. The journey may pause for a moment, but the journey of her soul never ends. It is a time in her life when one cycle is over and the next is about to begin. It is a time to savor her wisdom and admire the personal artwork of life she has created, because soon she will have to start the next cycle. A new beginning is found in the end. The pieces are now in place for her new journey to start.

The Devil Card
With the perspective of the Major Arcana as milestones of a life journey, the meaning of the Devil Card can now be interpreted in the broader context of Nicole's journey.

To understand the meaning of the card, let us first consider the more basic meaning of the Devil as a force of illusion and oppression. The main illusion in one's life is materialism. It is not just a financial concern, but a state of understanding that nothing exists beyond our five senses. In Nicole's case, the lack of awareness of the spiritual perspectives of life has led her material self to pursue her personal desires. This approach is narrow-minded and leads to unhappiness. So, very simply, the Devil card denotes the misery that is operating inside her.

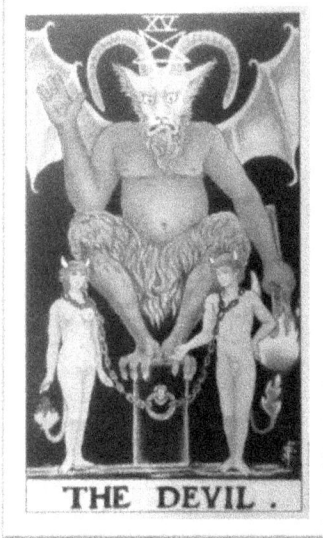

In the card, the Devil is noted to wear a reversed pentacle on his forehead. This indicates that the individual's desires are overruling his judgment. The card's background is black and the color symbolizes depression and inability to see the truth. It implies that the life energy is locked up in darkness. In this case, the Devil can mean a narrow materialistic view of life. It can also mean a form of misery or depression, feeling chained or imprisoned. This results in the illusion that no alternatives are available. The Devil signifies that the individual is being slave of his desires rather than acting the way he thinks best.

In many ways, I feel that Nicole's unhappiness has resulted from her giving in to personal desires, as the Devil card had indicated.

Day-To-Day Issues (Minor Arcana)
While the Major Arcana card meanings describe events that will naturally occur due to the laws of the universe, the Minor Arcana illustrates events that naturally occur because of human nature and highlights the more practical aspects of life. These are largely day-to-day issues which present to the individual with an opportunity to learn from these experiences.

The Minor Arcana consists of fifty-six cards in four suits:

(1) Suit of Cups – which represents the element of water. Water runs deep and our emotions and intuition run just as deep. Hence our emotions and intuition are closely associated with the suit of cups.

(2) Suit of Swords – which represents the element of air. Thoughts are the domain of the air element because air holds the unseen. The swords point a sharp tip to our fears, doubts and concerns, and the double-edged sword is akin to the dual-nature of the mind, as we have the potential to be "two-minded" about something.

(3) Suit of Wands – which represents the element of fire. Fire conveys heat, passion and ignition and so does the Suit of Wands, which brings the message of creative sparks, spiritual passion and social vitality in its images.

(4) Suit of Pentacles – which represents the element of earth and grounding energy. Material concepts such as the body, home and money all belong to this element or suit.

For the purpose of this book, I shall confine my description to the suits of Cups and Swords which Nicole had encountered in her meditation.

Suit of Cups – The cup is a water-containing vessel and this suit is representative of the element of water. In this suit, the emotional level of consciousness is associated with love, feelings and relationships. The drawing of a Cups card reveals a display of emotions or expression of feelings towards others. Cups are also linked to creativity, imagination and romanticism. The individual represented by the Suit of Cups (e.g. Queen of Cups) is, in general, emotional, artistic, humane and creative and will draw energy from how they feel within themselves.

Queen of Cups – The water in the cup indicates the nourishing of one's conscious life by one's unconsciousness. The card signifies the unity of the self with emotion and imagination. The individual does not feed his imagination by giving it complete freedom to wander. Instead he directs it into valuable activity. That the cup is being held by the Queen symbolizes the achievement obtained through imagination. Like all creative people, she derives inspiration for future activities through past experiences. Only love will give meaning to her actions and realize her goals. The goals are not simply creative, in the narrow sense of art, but also in the wider sense of making something wholesome. It includes emotional goals and family goals. She connects her consciousness to feelings. Hence, she knows what she wants and will take the steps to get it but also act with an awareness of love.

Suit of Swords – This suit is representative of action, change, force, power, ambition and courage. The action can be either constructive or destructive. The Suit of Swords deals with the mental level of consciousness, and centers on the mind and intellect. It mirrors the quality of the mind as represented by thoughts, beliefs and attitudes. As swords are double-edged, the suit symbolizes the balance between intellect and power and how these two qualities can be used for good or evil.

Page of Swords – As the Sword represents mental activity, the Page of Swords deals with mental conflict. He gets above them and detaches himself from them. The Swords signifies the cutting through of illusions and complicated problems. As the mind sees so many ideas and possibilities to a situation, understanding and action is sometimes impossible and the tendency is to stop thinking. However, the individual does not abolish a problem by banishing it. Rather he solves it by combining it with other elements. The more confusion he faces, the more he needs his mind because nothing else can sort out the truth for him. However, by combining Swords with Cups we combine the mind

with emotion and receptivity with the deep values grounded in psychological and spiritual truth. Then the problem of the cluttered mind changes to that of wisdom.

Interpretation of Nicole's Three-Card Spread
The Tarot has many layers of meaning embedded in the image components of each individual card. The challenge of interpreting a Tarot spread is not about coming out with descriptive words for the randomly selected cards, but about getting the individual to work with the combination of images to understand how their combined symbolism relates to his own life issues.

In Nicole's case, her familiarity with mindfulness and her ease of sliding into a meditative state enabled her not only to work directly with the cards, but to go beyond the simple awareness of each card. With the use of creative visualization she could act out multiple situations with the figures in the card. Under trance, she found her whole being present, and integrated as a part of the card experience. It was as if a fantasy was unrolling before her, while remaining aware of her trance state. What seemed enigmatic in the beginning had turned out to be an inspiring message. As Jung says, "Imagination is an organ of the subconscious," and when she was able to let go of herself and allowed herself to go where her mental imagery took her, she reached where her conscious mind would not have thought of or dared to go otherwise.

Each Tarot card image has its own designated symbolism, but it is something else when we see a combination of cards. Nicole's three-card spread has taught her a very important lesson about life and opened up a meaning that would not have emerged in any other way.

A fundamental feature of Tarot images is that they consist of a duality of opposites. The duality is often represented by the presence of male and female genders. The Page and the Queen in this instance is one such example. We also experience the duality more subtly in our daily lives – between our hopes and the reality of what we achieve. Very often, the choice one makes does not fulfill one's hopes. For Nicole, her medical career has not been what she wanted and her job has brought her more frustration than encouragement. Somehow, the reality of life is always less than the potential.

Nicole has been agonizing over her past decision. She has found difficulty accepting that, once she has taken a step forward in a particular direction, she seems to have lost the chance to go in all the other directions that were previously open. She has been unable to accept the limitations of working in the real world and could not see the perspective that her choice is one that can allow her to explore opportunities.

At the source of all these dualities, Nicole has been feeling that she does not know herself well enough. Deep down, she feels as if her true self is being buried within her normal, socially restricted personality. Yet the cards are telling her not to wait passively for an outside redemption agent, but bring to mind that it is her responsibility to find the key to the solution that she has been looking for.

The core message in this three-card Tarot spread is teaching her that key to unity and wholeness is really a process that comes through growth as she travels step by step through her life journey.

Devil between Page and Queen

The Page of Swords signifies mental alertness or sharpness and the sword represents intellectual or mental ability. In contrast, the cup represents the "water element" which signifies emotions and feelings. When both the Swords and the Cups appear in a journey of self-healing, it signifies that a certain part of Nicole, the part that deals with the balance between her heart and mind, needs to be awakened.

Nicole is aware that she has had issues in decision making. Although rational and practical by nature, she can be overly emotional, and many a time she has been torn between her heart and her head when making a decision. Hence the combination of the Page of Swords and the Queen of Cups describes her temperament closely.

PAGE of SWORDS.   THE DEVIL.   QUEEN of CUPS.

The Page of Swords represents an individual whose mental faculty cuts right to the heart of a matter. As a person, Nicole needs to expand her mind to look at things in new ways that she had not thought of before. The card combination is a reminder that once she understands the problem she is facing, she will, in her process of learning, find the answer rapidly.

The Queen of Cups represents Nicole's intuition and the richness of her subconscious mind. It also represents her emotion, desire, passion and inner healing power. These are qualities that she needs to nurture. When the Queen of Cups appears in the spread, it seems to be referring to the intuitive aspect of Nicole's personality, and suggests that she needs to think carefully about how she can better use her vast stores of spiritual wisdom. It is also a warning sign that she may be too involved with her heart and not thinking sufficiently with her head while she is facing her life issues.

The Devil card is a card of negativity and extremes and it signifies the "cancer" growing within the individual and devouring him from within. The presence of the Devil in the card combination seems to be indicating to Nicole that she has not been in control of her life. It is a life that has "turned upside down", in her own eyes. The warning message is that if and when she submits to forces represented by the Devil card, she is simultaneously submitting herself to every other force in the outside world that is harmful to her. Seen from the social perspective, she could be exposed to the danger of allowing others to control her life and bind her down. In a nutshell, the Devil figure probably symbolizes that part of her that needs healing.

In the first instance, when Nicole put the Devil figure in between the Page of Swords and the Queen of Cups, it obviously got in the way of the process of harmonization of her mental with her emotional energies. This resulted in the water, containing feelings and emotions (from Queen of Cups) being stained or polluted with blood (from the Devil).

Devil below Page and Queen

In the second instance, when Nicole allowed the Page of Swords and the Queen of Cups to come together, it represented the fact that she has recognized the importance of blending her masculine and feminine energies. In fact, the harmonization of the two polarities allowed the nurturing energy from the cup of water to pour onto the Devil and thereby allow healing and transformation to take place. The fact that the Devil lost his horns and transformed into a man-like character in Nicole's vision reaffirms that this is the intended life lesson for her.

The Circle, Arc and Straight Line

At Nicole's next meditation session, the divine message is simplified into three geometric figures: a circle, an arc and a straight line. The meaning appears straightforward.

The circle O is a symbol of the Sun and one's consciousness. It represents masculine, or Yang energy, that is bright, shining and illuminating. The combination of the arc and the straight line together forms the Moon.

The Moon represents feminine, or Yin energy. It is shadowy in its characteristics and symbolizes feelings and emotions. So this symbolic message sums up the fact that healing is about the balancing of energies from two opposing polarities, the mind (Sun) and the heart (Moon). This is what Nicole seriously needs for her personal transformation.

When the Devil gets in between, it was her mindset that became the critical obstacle. Whenever she believes that darkness has won, it has and she finds herself stuck. If she allows other people to determine how she should live her life, they will and she gets stuck. The truth is that if she can balance her mental and emotional energies, she will be able to make decisions on her own more effectively and move on in life.

CHAPTER ELEVEN

Paradox of the One and the Many

Dr. Nicole Lee

"People say that what we're all seeking is a meaning for life. I don't think that's what we're really seeking. I think that what we're seeking is an experience of being alive, so that our life experiences on the purely physical plane will have resonances with our own innermost being and reality, so that we actually feel the rapture of being alive."

Joseph Campbell
In: The Power of Myth

The subtle changes in me were coming alive. It was as if the boiling pot of frustration and angst in me was finally evaporating, and gradually being replaced by a sense of peace and calmness. I was consciously experiencing healing, but having been embroiled in imbalance and negativity for so many years, I needed more confidence and courage to effect the further changes for a more thorough transformation. And true enough; the next story that emerged from my subconscious mind empowered me with just what I needed.

Session 15 (Meditation): The Hunter and the Princess
It was Saturday morning, 14 June. As I commenced my meditation session in my usual manner, Tom and Lily promptly appeared before me, both dressed in their usual white robes.

I saw that the three of us were standing in front of a huge lake surrounded by tall mountains. From afar, I saw a tiny boat approaching us. As the boat neared us, I could see that there was no one on it. It stopped at the edge of the water just in front of me. Tom and Lily nodded their heads at me to get into it. I climbed into the boat, and it started to move back the way it came from, towards the opposite end of the lake hidden by the mountains.

I was feeling apprehensive in an unmanned boat, but Tom and Lily just smiled reassuringly at me and waved me on.

The boat glided smoothly across the calm waters. Soon, the water narrowed into a small stream between two steep mountain walls. I was entering a valley and I brushed my fingers along the rugged mountain walls that were so close to me. It felt so surreal!

After a while, I could see the valley ending. To my horror, the water now led to a steep waterfall ahead! I could hear the loud gushing sounds of free-falling water! I grabbed the sides of the boat, and my knuckles went pale. I could see the clear blue sky in the horizon. My fall was inevitable. I shut my eyes tight and braced myself for it.

The next moment, the boat fell off the edge of the waterfall and I hit the waters. The rapid river flow pushed me downstream, and as my head bobbed up and down, I was gasping for air. I saw a low-hanging branch overhead, and readied my body for the plunge upwards. I grabbed the branch, held on to it and hauled myself out of the water. Exhausted, I collapsed onto the riverbank.

I suddenly realized that I was a man this time! I held up my big strong hands, looking at them in awe. My body was tanned and strong, and I was dressed in brown leather clothes and leather boots. This was the first time I had appeared as a man in my meditation. However, I could not sense my identity or what I was doing for a living. It was a strange experience, but it certainly felt good to be strong. This was the reason why I was able to haul myself out of the rapids.

I rested a while, and surveyed my surroundings. I was in the middle of a dense forest. My instincts were sharp, and I could make out the trails made by the animals. It seemed that I had the senses of a hunter, and I dressed like one too. I decided to get out of the forest and head for the nearest town or village.

Instinctively, I was able to make out the trails and knew where to go. I walked for some time, and sure enough, I reached the end of the forest and saw a busy town ahead.

I headed into the town, and stepped into an inn to ask if there was work and lodging available. I was hungry and tired. The innkeeper looked at me with a strange expression, but he told me that I could rest in a room while he brought me some food. I sensed something might be amiss, but was too exhausted to heed my instincts. He directed me into a small room. After a short while, he served me some bread and soup, and I hungrily gobbled the food down. The next I knew, the room started spinning, and I lost consciousness.

I was not sure how much time had passed. My head felt heavy, and I slowly opened my eyes. I was no longer in the inn. Instead, I saw guards, and a man dressed in dark-brown uniform holding a baton standing in front of me. My hands were tied to the wall behind me. I was in a prison! The uniformed man was shouting something repeatedly, and it took me a while to figure out what he was shouting.

"Where is the gold? Where did you hide it?"

I had no idea what he was talking about. Having lost my memory, I could only shake my head in response. That earned me several beatings but I still could not recall anything. I was eventually thrown into a damp, musty cell.

The next morning, two guards tied my hands behind my back and led me out of the cell. As we exited the prison, I could hear the noises of a crowd. As we approached the exit, I saw a scaffold before me.

They were going to hang me!

I tried to struggle free, and several guards came upon me, and dragged me onto the platform. One of them forced the noose around my neck. I was furious and lashed out at them, but the noose only tightened around my neck.

All of a sudden, I heard a gunshot. The bullet cleanly sliced the rope from which the noose hanged. There was a masked person on a dark horse galloping through the crowd towards the platform. At the same time, the horses from the police stables ran amok into the crowd, causing a pandemonium. Someone had freed them earlier to create a commotion. The masked person signaled me to jump onto the horseback behind him. I kicked the guards next to me out of the way and jumped onto the horse as it passed by. We galloped away from the town into the forest. I looked back and saw the guards trying to grab the horses to chase after us, but to no avail.

We rode for some time through the forest and eventually stopped in front of a large cave. The person got off the horse, and cut my bound hands free with a knife. I got off the horse to thank my benefactor. To my surprise, when the person removed the mask, I found that she was actually a woman! She hugged me tightly and said that she was so happy to have saved me in time! However, I did not know who she was.

She brought me into the cave next. There were four other men standing around a fireplace. They turned when they heard us entering. I looked at them, and they appeared brutish and unkempt. One of them approached me and started asking me the same question that the soldier had asked earlier, "Where is the gold?"

I shook my head and replied that I did not know what he was talking about. His face contorted with anger, and he raised his fist. The woman quickly intercepted and said that I had just survived a near fatal event, and perhaps would be able to recall after a good night's rest. The man backed off reluctantly.

I felt unsafe. That night, I waited until they were drunk and had fallen asleep. I stealthily made my way out of the cave, and untied a black horse that they had tied to a tree. I quietly got on the horse and galloped into the forest. I knew they were likely bandits, and did not want to be anywhere near them.

I rode hard and fast. My hunter instincts enabled me to seek out the trails that led me further away from the cave. I decided to ride to the other end of the forest away from the town and the cave.

The night passed and the day dawned. I had been riding non-stop for several hours. I finally saw the end of the forest. Open grass plains lay ahead.

I rode into the plains, and could see a burned cottage and a barn at a distance away. I rode towards the barn to see if there was anyone I could ask regarding my current location. As I approached the barn, a young girl on a brown horse appeared out of the barn.

The sight of her shocked me!

At that instant, I realized that this young girl emerging from the barn was myself during my first therapy session (Chapter 1) – the Princess who left the English Castle for the Red Cottage! Also, I was actually the same man on the black horse who was chasing after the young girl during that same session!

How could this be possible? How could I be in two characters in two stories that eventually linked together?

Therapist's Note (22): On Subpersonalities
Dr. Peter Mack

Few of us ever pay attention to our inner complexities or our sense of "I-ness" and often take it for granted. The truth is that our sense of identity is an existential reality which can be experienced directly. However we tend to see it as one monolithic coherent unit and not as different parts.

There are in each of us a diversity of semi-autonomous subpersonalities, striving to express ourselves. A subpersonality is a synthesis of habit patterns, traits and complexes and other psychological elements around an inner urge which strives to be expressed and realized. The hunter and the princess in this session are examples. Under trance, these subpersonalities can be called up from the subconscious and appear in human form. They in turn become organized and synthesized around a higher order center which we call the "I".

Often, many of us are inclined to reject the idea. To some, the admission of the presence of subpersonalities is tantamount to a breakdown of their identity while others fear being implicated with the dissociated identity disorder. Intuitively we know that an essential unity underlies the myriad diversities of manifested life, but the personal aspect of this paradox is still not commonly accepted.

I was astonished and puzzled. I watched the sight of the young girl as she rode the horse across the plains away from me. I prodded my horse after her, hoping she could help with my queries. However, she seemed to quicken up, and I too gathered speed. As per the English castle story, she reached another town, and got off the horse hastily. I did not follow her into the town to avoid encountering any police or soldiers again. The last I saw was her leading the horse deeper into the town.

I rode away from the town further into the plains. I saw the same stream encountered by the princess from the English castle (where the young girl stayed for ten years and grew into the princess). I followed the stream into another forest and when the forest ended, the red cottage from the English castle story was there.

Tired and hungry, I approached the cottage. There was a small animal farm next to the cottage. The plump lady whom I encountered in the first therapy session was already here. (See Chapter 1 – At this time, the princess was still a young girl who had only just arrived at the castle.) She was as kind as I remembered her. I asked her for work and lodging, and she obliged with no hesitation.

From that day onwards, I stayed on in the red cottage and became the farm helper. I also hunted during my spare time to gather meat for our food.

A few years passed. One day, while I was out hunting in the forest, I heard a baby's cry. Someone had abandoned a baby boy in the middle of the forest! I rescued the poor child and brought him back to the cottage with me. The plump lady, as usual, accepted the boy as her own.

Ten years passed since the day I arrived at the cottage. The princess from the English castle turned up at the cottage one day. She eventually stayed on as well, and the four of us became an interesting family unit, bounded by choice, not blood.

My meditation session stopped here.

There had been an unexpected twist to the story. I was unable to figure out how and why I had appeared in two different characters in the same story, one as a strong hunter, and the other as a weak princess. I was puzzled! No matter how hard I thought about the story, I could not solve the mystery. I decided to get help.

Session 16 (Regression): The sequel to the Hunter and the Princess

Three days later, I turned up at Dr. Mack's clinic, shared with him this puzzling story from my subconscious, and asked for advice. After hearing my story, he decided that it would be worthwhile to pursue the case under regression.

Back on the therapy couch, I went into a trance state quickly after the initial breathing exercise. As I relaxed further, I heard an instruction from Dr. Mack: "Go to a safe place of your choice, a place of healing that you have chosen for yourself."

"It is my healing forest again. I am sitting on the grass," I said. "It is the same forest, and it has not changed. There is a stream in front of me, surrounded by trees. The biggest tree in the forest has a swing hanging from it."

"Stay in the forest and allow yourself to go deeper into your trance state. Next, go back to the time when you were a princess in the English castle. You are at the point when you have just left the castle and are now spending time with the family of a plump lady with a man and a child (Session 1) ... Are you there now?"

"Yes."

"Describe to me what you see."

"I am back in the cottage of the time when I first reached there. So we are now sitting at the table drinking soup and eating bread." As I was talking, I saw myself inside the body of the princess. "I am the princess now, and the hunter from the earlier story is at the table sitting diagonally opposite me."

"Go over and talk to him."

On that instruction, I tried to walk up to the hunter, but all of a sudden, I found myself in the hunter's body looking at the princess instead!

"I see myself as him now. It seems that I am shifting between the two characters, the hunter and the princess. Gosh ... It looks like I can be whom I want to be!"

"So you belong to both of them?"

"Yes ... but I cannot belong to both at the same time."

"So in other words, you can switch from one to the other. In which body are you in now?"

"I am now the hunter ... looking at the princess! She looks pale and weak. So they are in direct contrast. If I compare the two of them, one is tanned and one is pale; one is strong and one is weak. I sense I relate more to the princess, but I want to be the hunter."

Next moment I found myself continually switching identities between the two bodies. It was a most intriguing experience!

"I have just shifted back to the princess now looking at the hunter. He is a strong and tanned man, relatively reserved, and sharp," I continued.

"Do the princess and the hunter have names?"

"The word Clara comes to my mind for the princess, whereas the man is called Hanks. Now I am back to Hanks' body."

"Now leave the hunter, Hanks' body, and be yourself again. I want you to speak to both Clara and Hanks. Can you see both of them in front of you now?"

"Yes."

"Good. I want you to speak to Hanks, and ask him which part of your personality he represents."

I replied instinctively: "The part that I want to be."

"Turn to Clara and ask her the same question."

"The part that I am but do not want to be. For example, it has taken me so long to leave the castle. I have been pretending that I am strong but I am actually weak."

"Do you agree with that?"

I nodded my head slightly. "Yes, I agree that Clara is such a character, and so am I."

"Which part of you do you think Hanks represent?

"I have never sensed the masculine qualities in myself. But after experiencing the feeling of being in Hanks' body, it feels good to be strong, fast, sharp, and more importantly fearless and confident."

"So this is what you want to be? Have you ever succeeded before?"

"No. I have always been too fearful. Hanks, in contrast, is fearless."

"What is stopping you from becoming Hanks?"

"I am too tied down by restrictions and boundaries. I am also too concerned about what other people think."

Dr. Mack seemed persistent with his therapeutic approach. I sensed that he was trying to get me to learn from Hanks. "Ask Hanks how does he achieve what he wants to do, and how has he done it without being bound down by restrictions?"

"I think in his world as a hunter, he has to be fast and sharp to survive day to day. That is all he is concerned about – to survive the moment and the day. He does not think too far ahead, and he does not think of the past. Everything is about surviving the here and the now. He is also fearless. He can defend himself and he will not hesitate to do so. He relies only on himself. He does not harm others, but if others harm him he will retaliate. I really admire his ability to live in the moment, his confidence in his abilities, and the courage to stand up for himself."

"Is that something you can achieve for yourself too, given the correct environment?"

"But ... I don't know if such an environment exists in our modern world. There are just too many liabilities and worries. We always have to think and plan ahead to survive. I don't think it is possible to live like him in the current world."

"What makes you so sure that you cannot live like him?"

"He has no family and no strings attached. He has no encumbrance. He hunts and eats for the day. He doesn't plan or store ahead, unlike what most people have to do nowadays."

"So, Hanks is that part of you that you'd like to achieve but find it hard to be, whereas Clara is that part of you that is already inside you but you do not want to be? Perhaps you may want to …"

Before Dr. Mack could finish his sentence, I interrupted him because a new image was appearing.

"Dr. Mack … I think I am seeing the two of them standing in front of me now. I think they are merging together, but I cannot make out what or who the end product is."

There was a short pause and I heard a new set of instructions.

"Let them merge. But I want Clara to talk to Hanks and see how the two of them can merge together and yet function as one, even though their qualities are opposite, and see if there is a middle way out."

Before I could follow the instructions, I interrupted Dr. Mack again. "I also see Tom and Lily merging together to form my Higher Self!"

"Hmm … are they in front of you?"

"I was trying to see who the end product of Clara and Hanks is but I could not, and then I saw Tom and Lily merging together and the end product is my Higher Self."

It was fascinating.

Therapist's Note (23): On Anima and Animus
Dr. Peter Mack

Carl Jung has described two anthropomorphic archetypes of the unconscious mind. In each individual there is both a female and a male component of his inner psyche, but this is a theoretical construct and is not identical with the concept of gender.

Masculine energy is direct, dry, action-oriented, structured and firm, whereas feminine energy is moist, intuitive, receptive, wild and fertile. In Nicole, these energies are represented metaphorically by Hunter Hanks and Princess Clara as well as by Tom and Lily.

Human beings are psychologically androgynous. For the man who is developing his relationships, he must come to terms with emotions, vulnerability and needs. For the woman, she has to be more decisive and action-oriented while developing courage, power and wisdom in her development process.

Both men and women are on the path to their own integration and must struggle with the interpersonal ramifications of the anima and animus. In integrating the opposite energy components, Nicole needs to examine herself on her status of balance and decide what needs further development in her life. The key to controlling one's anima/animus is to recognize it when it manifests and differentiate the anima/animus complex from reality.

Basically, the anima is the unformed feminine that is forming within a man while the animus is the unformed masculine that is forming within a woman. An easy way to understand the concept is to visualize the Yin-Yang symbol of Harmony, in which anima is the black dot on the white side and the animus is the white dot on the black portion.

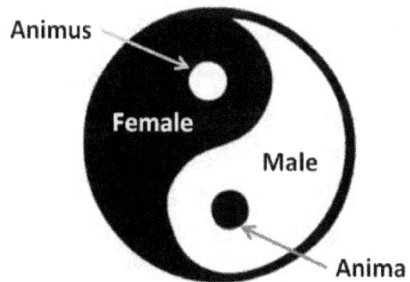

"Is the Tom-Lily combination separate from that of Hanks and Clara? Or are they one and the same?"

"They are separate, but I think they are trying to show me the merging of the male and female energies or the opposite qualities in an individual."

"What do you learn out of this?"

"Even though I may have the outward appearance of a female, I can have the desired male qualities that I never possessed and didn't know I wanted, until now."

"How do you think the merging of Hanks with Clara will produce the quality of the personality that will work for you?"

"Clara thinks too much, too far and always of the past. She is easily depressed and tends to sink into inactivity, whereas Hanks is the direct opposite. I think neither ends are feasible but a middle point will be good."

"Go deeper in your trance now ... and allow your subconscious mind to formulate a middle path for yourself that you believe is livable henceforth. Allow the middle path to emerge, and when you are ready to describe your experience, just speak up."

I took a deep breath, and a new scene gradually emerged.

"I see myself standing at a fork with three roads leading away from me. I know I should take the middle one."

"Where does the middle road lead you to?"

"I am walking down the path now and I see trees sprouting on the path."

"How do you make them sprout so fast?"

"They sprouted on their own." Suddenly, a flash of intuition came on. "Oh, I know where they are leading to!" I said. "It's leading me back to my healing forest!"

"So, are you back to your healing forest now?"

"Yes, I am looking at the swing now, standing from another angle."

"So what does the middle path leading you back to the healing forest mean to you?"

"I think there are more ways to reach the forest than the way I previously knew. All I have to do is to explore. It is like my home ground. Anytime I am lost, and need a place to go to, it is always there."

> **Therapist's Note (24): Using Subpersonalities in Therapy**
> **Dr. Peter Mack**
>
> Getting to know our subpersonalities is one of the easiest ways to facilitate personal growth. They are very much present in all of us, with each attempting to fulfill its own aims. Sometimes they cooperate, but more often they are a source of inner conflict. Often, they have some very beautiful and useful qualities that we may need, but may not be in touch with. As we understand our subpersonalities better we can regulate and direct their expression according to our own needs and goals. We can make them our allies and integrate them into a harmonious state. In regression therapy, recognizing their presence, directing them and dealing with them in the here and now usually enhances the sense of "I", or personal identity.
>
> When Nicole initially asked herself, "Who am I?" she would say, "I am Clara, the weak princess." After the therapy session she started saying, "I want to be Hanks, the strong hunter, but need to work harder to be like him." The visual merging of Hanks and Clara is a systematic way of harmonizing her masculine and feminine energies that would enhance her sense of identity and effectiveness in her outer world. Before this integration, she was limited by a particular subpersonality and by the inter-subpersonality conflicts. In such a situation, each subpersonality would want to control her and express itself, but often neither would yield. A deadlock would follow and energy would be wasted. But, as integration proceeded, it became possible to find a means of expression where both subpersonalities involved could get what they need.

Dr. Mack's questions came fast. "What does that translate to in terms of personal characteristics that you need to develop for yourself?"

"Besides the characteristics that I already know I have, there are others that I have not explored and if I do, they will help me onto my middle path."

"And what are those characteristics that you may want to explore, but which you have not done so?"

I took a deep breath before responding.

"To be emotionally stronger; to be able to live in the now instead of looking backwards or ahead all the time; to be more courageous and fearless; to dare to take risks; to be more confident of my own abilities and to trust my own instincts. All these are the qualities that Hanks had."

"Are you happy with the knowledge that once you have these qualities you will be able to move on satisfactorily in life?"

"Yes."

"Go deeper, and as you relax, imagine yourself staring at a tree within the forest …"

For a third time, I interrupted Dr. Mack because a new image appeared.

"Actually, I am now in Clara's body. We are at my healing forest. I am standing at one side of the stream looking at Hanks standing opposite me across the stream. Both of us start to enter into the water and walk towards each other. We hug each other. I know we are merging …"

"Good. Merge into each other and together you will share each other's qualities."

"Now, there is just me. I look into the water and I see my own reflection."

"How do you feel now? Do you feel you have all the qualities of Hanks at this stage?"

"I know they are in me. But I know it will take time and practice to bring them out, because Clara has been so overpowering over the years."

"Do you feel like bringing out these qualities in yourself now?"

Everything felt so new and unfamiliar to me, but I knew I wanted to have these qualities from now on.

"Yes," I said.

"I want you to imagine Hanks' qualities and abilities as a shape and give it a color. What do you see?"

"I see two colors, purple and yellow, twisted around like a rope."

"Use your mind to imagine this spiral keeps twisting around itself and let the rope get thicker and stronger. At the same time let the colors get brighter and brighter. Can you see that now?"

"Yes, the rope has transformed into a tree."

"So, this tree represents the qualities of Hanks in all its dimensions in terms of strength. At the count of three, you walk towards the tree and see yourself merging with it. One, two and … three. Henceforth all the qualities of Hanks are within you. Savor these abilities. See yourself as the tree and as it grows taller and wider as you become a giant, magnificent and an awesome tree."

Therapist's Note (25): On Integrating Subpersonalities
Dr. Peter Mack

Guided imagery is effective in getting at the underlying psychological drama of one's subpersonalities. This process is centered on creative visualization and represents a means of establishing a two-way communication between the conscious and the unconscious.

The images of a twisted rope with colors are of high symbolic value. By tapping into Nicole's unconscious mind, the creative visualization technique brought up the unconscious material in metaphors. This communication between the conscious and the unconscious improved the clarity of the direction of Nicole's values, goals and desired growth. It was her journey into the future.

The concept of subpersonalities also illustrates the Principle of Oneness. There is no need for any struggle or competition or for one part of the body to fight with another part. All that appears to be separate will in the end be an illusion to those who follow the path of separateness. Loss and gain is nothing but the spinning wheel of fortune that is based on the law of change.

The scene continued to evolve.

"I see myself growing bigger and wearing a soft, yellow robe that slowly turns into a purple color."

"Allow yourself to continue to grow bigger and bigger until you reach a size you are happy with. (pause) Have you reached your goal now?"

"Yes."

"With all the qualities integrated within yourself, you will be back to where you are here and now as a changed person as I count backwards from five to one. Five, four, three, two, one."

Our session ended and I opened my eyes.

It felt amazing how the stories of the princess and the hunter had merged to show me a valuable message! Suddenly a veil was lifted and something sacred was revealed yet again. Having experienced myself as the princess Clara, whom I had identified more with, I now had a clearer picture and understanding of how being weak and helpless would not help me in my current life in any way.

At this point in my healing journey, I needed the courage to brave the unfamiliar path ahead, and the confidence that I could do so. The experience as hunter Hanks with his positive qualities of courage, confidence, living in the now and trusting his instincts, had provided me with just the boost I needed to move on, and integrate the lessons imparted to me into my daily life. Without courage, confidence and the trust in my instincts, none of the messages would truly hit home and become part of my spiritual fabric. The story in this healing session could not have been timelier.

CHAPTER TWELVE

A New Beginning

Dr. Nicole Lee

"The two most important days in your life are the day you are born and the day you find out why."

Mark Twain

One of my secret ambitions in life is to be an author, but I had always somehow dampened my own enthusiasm and crushed any budding ideas because I had never believed in myself.

For the past month, after every healing session, be it one of regression or meditation, I would furiously write in my journal about the images and messages I had experienced. After the last and particularly insightful session, it suddenly occurred to me that this interesting and insightful content could be of help to others who were in similar situations to myself.

The thought of documenting my healing journey as a book suddenly came to mind. I was excited and quickly connected with Dr. Mack to explore the idea. It turned out that he was extremely supportive. He actually had been toying with the same idea, but knowing that I was a private person, had chosen to wait for an opportune moment to propose the idea. Indeed, I had been a private person. I did not have any Facebook, Twitter, Instagram or any other social media accounts. Hence, I felt that my very decision to write this book was itself a personal breakthrough.

The pieces of my life were coming together. Over the past weeks, the invaluable spiritual messages that I had received had initiated my inner healing. They helped to bridge the gap that existed between the outer material world and my inner spiritual self. However, the final puzzle was waiting to be pieced together. I could sense that I was close to finding my purpose of life.

Session 17 (Meditation): The Treasure Chest

> *"We all have a divine mission on earth. Let that mission be to inspire love and embrace the light within. Let that mission be to have peace in our hearts as we create heaven on earth. Let that mission be to seek empowerment through transformation and to breathe joy into everything we do. If we allow these things to be our mission the golden light of the sun will shine on our souls and change our world forever."*
>
> *Michael Teal*

It was 20 June, exactly a month after I started therapy. My family members had started to sense changes in me as a person. On my part, I felt that I had begun on a journey and there was no turning back.

I calmed my mind and meditated. I knew I was ready to explore the answer to my purpose in life. As trance set in and got deeper, I found myself standing in front of a large lake.

The water surface of the lake was tranquil and stillness in the air prevailed. As I continued to stare at the water, I noticed that the water level had started to drop, and the lake appeared to be drying up rapidly. As the water level dropped further, I could make out something was appearing in the middle of the lake. It was a chest! Soon, the lake was dry, and all that remained was a deep crater with the chest in the middle of it.

I descended along the slope of the crater, and walked curiously towards the chest, with my heart pounding at the excitement of what could lie inside. It was an old wooden chest, very much like those that frequently appeared in treasure hunts. I took a deep breath to focus my mind, because I knew that whatever was inside would provide the answer to my question.

Slowly, I lifted up the chest lid. To my amazement, there was the largest and most luminescent pearl I had ever seen! I cupped the pearl with both my hands and cautiously lifted it out of the chest. As I did so, its light shone brighter, and cast a hemispherical hologram screen around me.

I heard a voice saying, "What is the question you want to ask?"

I replied: "What is the purpose of my life?"

In the next instant, I saw the following six words flash across the hemispherical screen in front of me: "*To Lead, To Help, To Awaken.*"

The luminescence from the pearl started to fade, and the pearl transformed into a piece of white paper in my hands, folded into two halves. I knew instinctively that the contents of the paper contained a further clue to my question.

I slowly slid one side of the paper down to reveal what was inside. An unfamiliar symbol appeared – it contained three straight lines, a semicircle plus a crescent.

I stared at the symbol for some moments but could make no sense of it. I decided to seek my spiritual guides' help as I believed it held the important clue to my life quest!

Instantly Lily and Tom appeared before me, smiling as if they already knew I needed help.

Lily pointed to the chest, which was now closed, and told me to open it again. I gladly followed her instructions, but instead of the pearl, I saw my blue journal book that I had been using to document the experiences of my healing journey! She instructed me to place the book on top of my head and not to let the book fall off.

I was perplexed by her instructions but followed them. I placed the journal on my head, and instinctively stretched out both my arms horizontally to balance myself.

Suddenly, the image of me with a book on my head and horizontally outstretched arms balancing on a hemisphere which was in turn placed on a crescent, flashed across my mind. This was what the symbol meant: To balance!

It finally struck me that this was my long-awaited epiphany!

My life purpose is to seek a balance between the four dimensions – the physical, mental, emotional and spiritual aspects of my life. In turn I should lead, help and awaken others to also lead a more balanced life. The world today seems to constantly throw us out of balance and no matter what we do, we still feel as if life is going the wrong way. With balanced living, we will have a handle on the various elements in our life and won't feel that our heart or mind are being pulled too hard in one direction. We will be able to enjoy every moment of our life, experience happiness, offset negative events with positive ones and love the person we are.

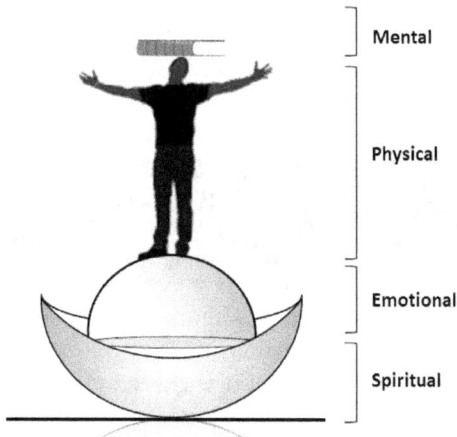

The four dimensions of living were all integrated into the symbol. The book, as represented by the first horizontal line of the symbol, connotes intellectual activity and refers to the mental dimension of our existence. The human figure with the outstretched arms, as represented by the cross, signifies the material tasks and challenges we need to deal with daily and refers to the physical dimension. The semicircle refers to the emotional dimension which represents the bridge that links our mental and physical dimensions with the spiritual dimension. Finally, the spiritual dimension is represented by the crescent, which forms the foundation of the symbol. Without a spiritual perspective in my life all the other three aspects will never be in true balance!

For the past ten to twenty years of my life, I had engulfed myself completely in coping with the material routines of daily living, pursuing intellectual challenges and battling against negative emotions. I had never taken a step back and truly connected with my spiritual essence until the start of the current therapy experience. I hung on to my past despite my unhappiness, and distracted myself with mundane physical activities because, inwardly, I thought that moving on would negate all that I had worked hard and suffered for, and counteract all my coping mechanisms that I had painstakingly developed to "protect" myself.

Alas, how wrong of me!

Therapist's Note (26): The Holistic Paradigm of Wellness
Dr. Peter Mack

The prevailing paradigm in conventional Medicine is the model of restorative therapeutics, whereby the health professional intervenes to restore the patient to a prior state of functioning. Central to this paradigm is that disease is an unavoidable state and can only be remedied by drugs, surgical ablation, radiation or genetic modification. The aim of medical treatment is to restore the patient's state to where he is before the problem.

In contrast, the holistic health model aims for a dynamical change in the individual and his life system. It brings insights from the meaning of his illness and applies it to transform his life system. The aim is to help the person develop new resources so that he may use the experience of illness consciously to bring his life to a greater level of awareness and appreciation. This approach acknowledges the existence of an inherent wisdom in the individual's body, mind, soul and spirit. It also motivates him to develop an ability to thrive under harsh circumstances, contribute to others and to fulfill a higher purpose in life.

The central tenet in holistic healing is that personal change rarely comes directly from the area in the physical body that is wounded or diseased. Instead, it comes if and after the individual acknowledges the wound and discovers how he has caused further pain for himself in his attempt to disconnect himself from the source of illness. Through this process he understands how his health is anchored to tension and stress. He transforms himself by associating with whatever seems like a source of pain and perceives it as a source of opportunity. He redefines himself through empowered actions and dissolves limiting ideas that obstruct his life journey. At the next stage he awakens to the experience of effortless being and knowing. As he advances in his wellbeing, he revisits his previous experience and learns how to choose his combination of resources better in various circumstances in future.

I finally understand why and how polarity exists in this world. It is to promote the learning of life lessons. Without experiencing the imbalanced way of living in my earlier life, I would never know what balanced living is; much less help anyone else achieve it. I also realize that the events in my life occur in such a way that I am being exposed to the lessons that are necessary for my soul's evolution. It is wonderful to understand that there is no need for regret. Everything happens for a reason. The truth may take time to surface, sometimes decades later.

Everything seems to have fallen into place. I am grateful that for once, I have not ignored the urge to follow my heart in producing this book. The writing process has consolidated my learning and given me access to the "mirrors" of my subconscious mind. I can feel myself healing and blossoming. If any of the messages and stories in my healing journey have also resonated with my readers in their own life journeys, the purpose of this book will have been fulfilled.

Every day since then, I have sought to remind myself that I am first and foremost, a spiritual being. I am not here just to engage in physical tasks and mundane thinking, worrying over my regretful past and uncertain future or getting depressed about them. Once in harmony with my spiritual nature, I will be able to explore the deeper meanings underlying my existence in the physical world, and see that no event is inherently good or bad, but how it is actually crafted for the learning and evolution of my spiritual self.

Once we are awakened, all it takes is a little more effort every day to be mindful of cultivating our spiritual nature, and maintaining the balance between the four dimensions of our individual selves. What can be more meaningful and fulfilling than leading a purposeful life?

CHAPTER THIRTEEN

Purpose of Life

Dr. Peter Mack

"The purpose and point of this life is to learn and love – and it may be more specifically to learn to love."
Kimberly Giles
In: *Choosing Clarity: The Path to Fearlessness*

One frequent source of anxiety among patients coming for therapy is their inability to find meaningfulness in their lives. They often wonder if they have found their life purpose, and if not, whether they have been mismanaging their lives without their awareness. The lack of a direction prompts many of them to ask if regression therapy could assist in their search for life's true meaning, regardless of whether they are blessed with physical health and abundant lifestyle.

Probably most of us would not have thought about our existential purpose, until we encounter a major illness or a turning point in our life. Many of us would have blundered through life, doing what we were told by our parents and seniors or conforming to what other people do. Now and again, our society would toss fragments of meaning at us and we may pick a choice from among these fragments to create our own set of messages, making it coherent and consistent. Yet, most of us would share the sentiment that creating the meaning of one's life is not at all easy.

Like many others, Nicole has been experiencing her life as one that is full of suffering. She has been through tough times, and this has left her lost in the dark. Deep down, she has been filled with a vague and pervasive sense of emptiness and wondered if life has any meaning at all. However, she is not alone. All too often, most of us experience difficulty understanding the real nature of life. This is because of our own ignorance and strong desires.

Most of us have our individual life goals. The kind of goals that the majority of us have in mind are predominantly worldly in nature, like struggling to ace our exams, winning a competition, getting accepted into a prestigious university course, a successful romance, a steady job, buying a residential apartment, becoming rich and famous, or representing one's profession in a certain field. Our entire education system today is set up to help us pursue these worldly goals. When we become parents we instill the same worldly purpose in our children by encouraging them to study and enter professions that give them a brighter career future. However, most of us have overlooked that these life goals are relevant only for the time being. They are a means to an end and not the end in itself.

There is a difference between ever-changing life goals and an unswerving purpose that explains what we are born to do. The satisfaction of achieving our life goals is short-lived. We soon realize that the acquired happiness quickly disintegrates, fades into a memory and turns into reminiscence. This puts us back on the starting line, and sets us on to identifying our next goal to work towards. In contrast, the satisfaction of realizing life's purpose neither withers nor fades.

Those of us who have ever absorbed ourselves in our favorite activity, be it career development, sports competition or a hobby, would have experienced the feeling of deep satisfaction. We might even have thought that this could be the very reason why we feel alive and motivated. Yet, these activities cannot be considered as our true purpose of life. Deep within, we still encounter emptiness even after our dream has been fulfilled. With time we find the satisfaction of our achievement transforming into a mental memory, and we need to set our next goal to feel alive and driven.

Where then do we search for the purpose of life?

From the philosophical perspective, all human beings are born for one purpose only. It is to search for happiness. In a world where everything perishes, the search for imperishable happiness is our common desire. Hence, its attainment may be considered our life's true purpose.

But many people would ask: Isn't life one of eternal suffering? And if so, how is happiness possible? Indeed, through deep contemplation some of us may have discovered that life and suffering are indeed inseparable. There is not a single individual in this world who is free from physical, emotional or mental pain. Everything pertaining to our life is subject to change and non-satisfactoriness. Hence, as long as there is craving for worldly pleasures or desires for existence, we are unable to escape from suffering.

So, can happiness and pain coexist?

I believe the answer lies in whether one knows the cause of one's suffering. Suffering always stems from our basic passions and desires. If a person has no desires, or if he is not striving for position, authority or wealth, then he is unlikely to experience sorrow. In other words, suffering will cease if he has no attachment to worldly things, feels contented and focuses his thoughts on higher values. However, such a state of mind is not easy to attain.

Desire is fundamental to our nature and existence. When existence takes place, suffering is unavoidable. Whatever happiness we can obtain is usually secured amid many disappointments, failures and defeats. There simply isn't a life where there are no difficulties, conflicts or problems. The more we struggle to escape from unpleasant situations the more we entangle ourselves with problems.

Yet, as individuals we are not designed to put up with that which we find unpleasant. We are meant to change it. Accepting suffering and hardships as an opportunity for learning and reflection is a path to happiness, but it is also a hard lesson. It takes time and effort for an individual to appreciate that the causes of one's emotional pain does not lie with other people in the outside world, but actually within oneself. By asking ourselves what is the lesson that we can learn from our pain and suffering, we can uncover the seed of our happiness. Every twitch of pain invites us to wake up to look for a grander truth. The moment we get a glimpse of a higher, overarching reality and a more magnificent self, we come closer to an awareness of our true place in the universe.

Purpose of Life

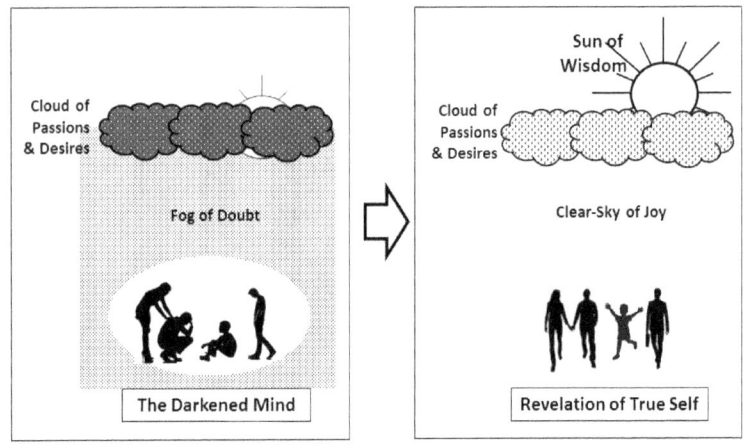

What then is the purpose of our life?

Well, the answer becomes more obvious once the darkness of our mind is eradicated. It is akin to a rising sun of wisdom, which shines through the cloud of passion and desires, to dispel the fog of our mental doubt. Without the sun, the individual will have no way of knowing of the presence of the cloud and fog. Nor would the darkness itself be perceived as such. The individual will now realize that the activities, goals and things that have been making life pleasurable for him are all simply a means for revealing his true self. This is so that he acquires the self-knowledge to work towards a higher purpose.

Life therefore has a definite purpose – it is to have one's darkness of mind dispelled. When mental darkness disappears, the naked self is revealed. The individual knows that he is driven by passions such as jealousy and envy. No matter how thick are the clouds and fog that cover the sky, as long as the sun is shining, there will be light underneath the clouds. One gets enlightened when one sees clearly that one's true self is composed of nothing but blind passions and desires.

From the worldly perspective, self-revelation refers to perceiving the physical, mental and intellectual qualities and defects in oneself. We have noted earlier that success in the material world is defined by the acquisition of respect, money, fame, career achievements, power etc. From the metaphysical viewpoint, success is about making spiritual progress. The revelation of one's true self in the spiritual sense would lead to the realizing that "I am the God within and am experiencing it."

How can we liberate ourselves from our darkened mind?

It is simply a process of awakening. This process is analogous to the experience of dreaming. A person may dream that he is running desperately for his life away from a wild beast, only to wake up, drenched in sweat, to discover that it has all been a dream. While he is dreaming, he is unable to know that he is dreaming. Therefore, the moment of awakening comes only when he emerges from his sleep state and becomes aware of both the reality and the dream at the same time.

Let us now examine our life purpose from a developmental perspective. As part of the human race, we are collectively on a journey of evolution. This means that the life that each of us is going through is an adaptation process. As an individual being, we choose the environment we want to survive in and find meaning in the way we adapt to the harsh circumstances we encounter. In this way we make progress in our development. This concept of human evolution is fundamental to understanding the meaning of life.

By adapting to our environment, we survive, make changes and become stronger in ourselves. No matter how harsh life appears to us, we can from this very moment onwards see it more positively, make it better, and create the outcomes we want. Things will get increasingly better with time, and become a joy to experience. Life will then be worth living.

As such, the purpose of life is dependent on the way we use it to improve ourselves. If we are paralyzed by our painful past and succumb to our human weaknesses, no purpose is served. Nothing worthwhile will be achievable. If we choose to satisfy our physical desires as the purpose of our life, then we must be prepared to face various problems arising therefrom. On the other hand, if we act wisely, cultivate our virtues and exercise our patience, tolerance, kindness, sympathy and humility, and render service to others, we are more likely to achieve something noble and meaningful. Harmony, happiness, calm and peace will follow and we will find life more worthwhile. The more our life goals are in line with the intent of spiritual development, the richer our lives become and the less pain we experience.

How then do we know that we have found our life purpose? The knowing is a self-evident process. In Nicole's case, when she started to see and do things that supported her life purpose, she began to experience the reception of a positive feedback. Things suddenly progressed in a more favorable manner. She experienced fulfillment with the fact that she was making a difference to her life. Knowing that something good will come of her efforts and that her close ones will appreciate her more, had made make a tough job more meaningful and easier to bear. Chance coincidences seemed to be occurring in close succession. These occurrences supported her goals and projects, and her efforts were producing results more readily. These served as a reminder and confirmation that she was on the correct path. She called these events synchronicity or serendipity. They were representations of the universe's way of providing feedback that she was moving in the right direction.

Through her healing journey, she gained insights into the distinctions between her ego and her soul. Her ego has divided her life experiences into likable and dislikable categories, and she had been craving for likable life circumstances so as to be free from pain and struggle. On the other hand, her soul was more concerned with *being* rather than doing, and had no attachment to the physical form in which she would manifest her purpose.

Her soul did not divide experiences into good and bad categories. Instead, her soul saw her life as a learning journey rather than a destination to get to. By getting onto her soul path, she has learned that she will grow from her experiences, regardless of whether she likes them. In a nutshell, the purpose of one's life boils down to the spiritual development of one's soul. The physical environment of an individual's life on Earth is intended to be a "schoolroom" for his soul to learn his lessons, according to his Life Plan.

APPENDIX I

Imagination, Imagery and Healing

Dr. Peter Mack

"What is its (imagery's) function in terms of human survival and happiness? The answer must be given in evolutionary terms, both the species and for the individual. Imagery permits the exploration of various possibilities for action without the time constraints and possible dangers of the real event."

Robert Sommer
In: The Mind's Eye: Imagery in Everyday Life

The manner in which Nicole arrived at an understanding of her life purpose resulted from the use of a unique blend of regression and mindfulness approaches. She had rapidly mastered her technique of creative visualization and emerged with a series of pertinent imagery. To distill the meaning out of these images, she meditated over them repeatedly to receive guidance from the universe. This turned out to be an effective way of healing.

The technique of mental imagery is intrinsic to the practice of regression therapy. An established approach for exploring new realms of the unconscious mind, it brings the individual into a journey of discovery by using the imagination under the direction of the conscious intellect and the will. Nicole was able to shift gears, back and forth at will, between the direct, creative experience of her inner world and the more rational analytic framework of her outer consciousness.

The guided imagery approach begins by posing a conscious question to one's unconscious mind and allowing the answer to emerge in the form of a mental image. The mind takes an expectant mode while being simultaneously relaxed, receptive and goal-directed. The situation is analogous to watching a movie and waiting for the film characters to appear in action on the screen. Given sufficient attention, the significance of the emerging imagery will become clear, after some reflection, if not immediately.

In the earlier stages of healing, Nicole had expressed doubts and uncertainties with regards to the level of reality of guided imagery. She asked if she had "imagined" the imagery that appeared while she was under trance and if there was a possibility that she had been "hallucinating" during the therapy. I was alerted to her concern that she might have unconsciously "falsified" all her mental imagery, thus "kidding herself" in the process. My immediate reaction was a straight "no". However, she needed an intellectual explanation, and the intellectual response required to meet her needs was less straightforward. This was simply because her issue begot a bigger question: "What exactly is imagination?"

What is Imagination?
Imagination is a very complex and loaded concept that has radically different meanings when used in different contexts. Unfortunately, it is a common misconception that imagination is a form of illusion and self-deception.

Many of us draw a sharp contrast between the world of imagination and the real world. We tend to use phrases like "figments of imagination" to imply the product of the imaginative process as fantasy or being shadowy. Medical undergraduates commonly encounter the term in their clinical psychiatry rotation and are thus inclined to assume that imagination is a pathological and non-respectable process.

The psychological literature on imagination is replete with theories, controversies and ambiguities. It has given many people the impression that the concept of imagination has an air of the unscientific about it and renders it suspect to medical professionals who pride themselves on their rationality. Yet the world of imagination does not take us away altogether from the real world. There is in fact a good deal in our conscious awareness of the real world that is contributed by imagination.

Imagination is our capacity to form mental images, analogies, objects or events in the absence of stimulation of brain receptors. The mental images so formed are usually of a visual nature, but may occur in combination with other forms of perception such as sound, smell and touch.

Imagination may also be viewed as the ability of an individual to call forth mental pictures of absent individuals, objects, or situations at will. The process involves the reorganization of data derived from past memory or experiences into a new mental pattern. The new pattern so formed is the result of a synthesis of various aspects of experiences or memories into a mental construct. This construct differs from the perceived reality of the past. It can be something fanciful, or even wishful. Yet, when imagination is applied in the context of regression therapy, it often translates into a powerful problem-solving process for the patient.

With this understanding, I would reply to Nicole that the narrative experience she went through in her therapy, indeed matches the characteristics of an imaginative process.

But, were her guided narratives "real" or "fake"? To this end, I feel there needs to be a distinction between the concepts of imagination, illusion and hallucination.

Hallucination

Both illusion and hallucination are errors of perception. An illusion occurs when an individual sees an object in a form other than what it is supposed to be. So, it is simply a process of deception in which a misleading impression of reality has been produced. On the other hand, a hallucination occurs when an individual sees an object that is simply non-existent. In other words, there is no visual stimulus to start with.

So how does hallucination differ from imagination, since both are mental creations in the absence of real-world stimuli?

There are several features of the hallucinatory experience that have no exact counterparts in the imaginative process.

Firstly, most hallucinations are associated with mental pathology or psychiatric disease. Strong accompanying emotions such as anxiety, paranoia or fear are usually present. In addition, hallucinatory images tend to be very vivid and rich in the quality of their appearance, so much so that the individual believes that the image content is real. This may happen to the extent of distorting and rivaling the normal process of perception.

In contrast, imagination is an inherently innocent process. It neither distorts nor rivals normal perception. The imagined object or event is clearly distinguished from its real-world counterpart. The imaginative process does not, in any way, involve a belief in empirical reality.

Unlike the negative emotions surrounding hallucinatory images, the mental imagery used in regression therapy is often accompanied by awe, meaningfulness and insightful experiences. For example, the English castle that Nicole visualized lacks the pictorial richness and power to make her believe that she has actually stayed there for ten years. Yet the metaphorical richness of the story provides a fertile medium for the discovery of her source of emotional difficulty. This leads to her understanding of the motivational forces behind her thoughts, actions and attitude, and eventually to healing.

Secondly, hallucinations tend to arise spontaneously and are beyond the individual's conscious control. They often appear so rapidly and with little warning that the individual tends to be shocked and disturbed at what has happened.

In contrast, no such disturbing situations occur in imagination. The surprise element in imaginative images is characteristically of a mild nature and the individual has an ability to control and terminate the images at will. In regression therapy, the imaginative process is guided and somewhat anticipatory in nature, while the experience itself is often pleasant, fascinating or of a revealing nature.

Guided Imagery

By "guided imagery" I am referring to a therapeutic approach involving creative visualization, which is being used all the time by regression therapists. By guiding the patient through the visualization process it helps the individual to create images and stories that amplify the positive aspects of the mind-body connection. This helps to uncover the inner truth about the patient.

Guided imagery encompasses a range of therapy techniques including simple visualization and direct imagery-based suggestion through the use of metaphors and story-telling. At the heart of the technique, it is a form of creative imagination that improves communication between the conscious and the unconscious mind.

The practice of creative imagination is not new. Man has long sought contact with his inner psyche through the use of mental imagery. The use of induced dreams is one such method and it evokes the symbolic potential of the psyche. Primitive peoples have long applied the practice of provoking dreams to seek guidance for an important decision or healing of an illness. They do so by establishing contact with an archetypal healing image that could provide this help.

The vision quest of South American Indian tribes is another example of creative imagination. The individual would practice fasting and other kinds of austerities in isolation until he obtained a vision of his totem animal. I recall encountering a patient who told me of his unexplained and immense liking of animals in the dog family since childhood. In one of his therapy sessions, he regressed back to a past life as a native American Indian who, on his vision quest, was canoeing and tracking up the jungle one evening and met a wolf as his totem animal.[10] The meeting of the totem animal under trance provoked intense catharsis and immediately initiated his healing process.

Historically, the first use of mental imagery in therapeutic work was by Pierre Janet in the 1890s. He used the technique of substituting one image for another in hysterical patients who had fixated ideas. In psychotherapy work, Carl Happich developed the approach of using predetermined scenes such as a meadow, a mountain or a chapel as "points for departure" in the 1920s. His patients would undergo the prescribed visualization repeatedly, a meadow for instance, until they were able to experience positive symbols (e.g. blossoming flowers) and eliminate negative ones (e.g. a rotting stump) in the meadow.

Other pioneers of mental imagery were Pierce Clark, who found the use of fantasy useful, while Anna Freud later used both free and guided imagery in her work with children. Later, Carl Jung developed the method of "active imagination", which included not only visualization but also other techniques such as painting, writing, dancing and acting. In the 1940s, Desoille used mental imagery in his waking-dream method by getting the patient to imagine various scenes of rising or descending in an imaginal space. This approach is evocating to the patient's higher ethical and spiritual tendencies as he rises. The images of ascent frequently led to archetypal celestial beings and experiences of a mystical nature which are strengthening to the patient. Healing in such a situation could be obtained by symbolic ascent. In later years, Andre Virel and Roger Frétigny developed their approach called "oneirotherapy" (from the Greek word "oneiros" meaning dream). In their approach emphasis is placed on relaxation and attention is given to integrating the imagery sessions with the patient's life situation.

---

[10] An animal totem is a teacher and spiritual guide. It is often an animal to whom one feels a close connection in some period of one's life. This particular past life story is described in detail in the book by the author: *Life-Changing Moments in Inner Healing, 2002*

The mental imagery used in this book involves the additional use of dialogue. For each session I work with whatever theme that Nicole has proposed. Rather than suggesting any starting image, I allow her to have a spontaneous image that appears on her mind screen. This has consistently turned out to be a "healing forest". It opens the way to a next step to elucidating the theme that she wants to explore. I allow a free flow of her imagery to take place and encourage her to contact whatever or whoever is important in that moment. This often results in a peak experience coming on, in its own time, when she is ready.

Relating what takes place at the symbolic level to the patient's everyday life is an important element of the therapy. It is particularly useful to integrate this process within the session itself. For this reason, I tend to facilitate the eliciting of detailed imagery that helps Nicole see how the themes of the images are expressed in her current life. For this reason I specifically draw her attention to the parallel between the "three outcomes" (in Session 9) and her decision-making ability in her current life.

One hallmark of the use of guided imagery in regression therapy is to tap into the wisdom of the patient's creative consciousness. With Nicole I have allowed the spontaneous unfoldment of the imagery of her spiritual essence in the form of a Higher Self. This provides the platform for the wisdom of the healing messages to be brought forth in a manner most suited to her needs. Insights obtained from the material of the unconscious, largely in the form of metaphors, are brought to the light of consciousness. It remains for her to draw the conclusions from her insights to integrate into her life.

In Session 2, I have used guided imagery to help Nicole resolve her grief over the plight of being coerced by her mother into entering medical school against her wishes. The mental imagery provides a cognitive structure for her to relive the scene of sorrow, and re-grieve over the unfortunate event. It also allows her to revise the experience to recreate scenes of what could have otherwise happened. This approach helps her to reconstruct her future-oriented identity. By integrating the technique with psychodrama, in which she could interact with her mother under trance, the technique brings out the very tears that she wanted to shed at that time of the earlier event, but never did. The outcome of the therapeutic maneuver is dramatic and rapidly changes her view of reality concerning her grieving process.

Healing with Guided Imagery
The concept of "healing" used in this book is broader in scope than that of "curing" as used in Medicine. While the term healing embraces the concept of finality to a disease state or the correction of a physiological disturbance, it includes a wider concept of wholeness in the patient. This state of wholeness has many dimensions. It includes those aspects of health that involve an increased capacity for love, compassion, forgiveness and soul growth, all of which are functions of the unconscious mind.

Guided imagery provides an ideal environment for the therapist to work with the content of the patient's unconscious mind. The patient can relax deeply and enter into a trance state and yet, at the same time, work with a reductionist mode. It is a marvel that under trance, a patient can analyze the most basic mechanisms that are in operation in a complex situation, and at the same time be able to synthesize components that make up the situation. This synthetic mode is the ability to rearrange the individual parts that are at work together to generate the complexity into new wholes that would provide new perspectives in meaning.

Learning new meaning is an integral part of healing. In an altered state of consciousness, or under trance, the patient is usually more capable of experiencing rapid learning, growth and healing. Intuition and creativity are often enhanced. Mood and cognition can undergo change. In this state, the patient is able to do things that he cannot do in a normal wakeful state. This is because the altered state provides a phenomenal source of internal strength for healing.

Besides bringing the content of the unconscious mind into the light of consciousness, the therapist also helps the patient assume responsibility for what his unconscious minds reveals and integrate the material into his life. Ultimately healing involves not only the conclusions drawn from the material of his unconscious, but also the application of the insights to his daily living.

In short, healing involves the need for communication between the conscious and the unconscious, and guided imagery is a vehicle for facilitating that communication. What has been unique in Nicole's case is her ability to visualize her Higher Self through meditative techniques.

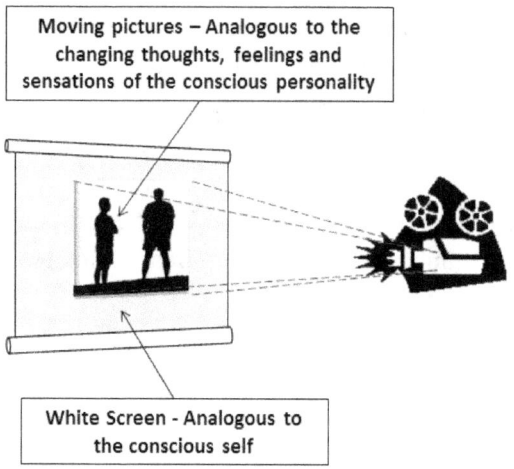

The concept of the Higher Self has been explained in Chapter 3. When people speak of the Higher Self, they generally confuse it with the knowing or awakened aspects of themselves, the "I", or the "conscious self". The true Higher Self is unaffected by the flow of the sensations, thoughts and feelings of the mind-stream of the conscious self.

The "I" or conscious self is analogous to the white area on a projection screen, whereas the changing content of the conscious personality, namely the sensations, thoughts and feelings, are like the pictures projected upon the screen. The conscious self should not be mistaken as the Higher Self. The conscious self disappears altogether when we fall asleep, faint or are being anesthetized. When we are awake, the conscious self mysteriously reappears.

In spiritual literature, the Higher Self is referred to as an eternal, omnipotent, conscious and intelligent being that is within all of us. It is a spiritual essence through which the integration of a person's learning with his personality takes place. Every one of us has a blueprint or divine template that holds information about every single atom of our being. The function of the Higher Self is to help us gain access to the information residing in this blueprint.

In summary, the Higher Self is the more complete version of the self. It is the one that is not being frustrated by the veil that draws upon us when we incarnate and that causes us to forget where we come from. It is watching over us and helping us to steer us in the direction we intended to go when we create our Life Plan. The Higher Self is right here with us. Connecting with and mentally imaging the Higher Self is not a difficult task. It can be done in a mindfulness state, and creative imagination is the key.

APPENDIX II

The Soul in Reincarnation

Dr. Peter Mack

"Reincarnation contains a most comforting explanation of reality by means of which Indian thought surmounts difficulties which baffle the thinkers of Europe."

Albert Schweitzer

Why does the soul wish to reincarnate? Why would it, in the perfectly happy spirit realm, want to inhabit a physical body with all its limitations and difficulties?

It is precisely because the body form has its restrictions that the soul would want to inhabit the physical realm. Only through a vehicle will the soul experience the reality of what it feels like to be separated from other souls, and not being in a state of perfect, unconditional love at all times. Every soul reincarnates for a specific purpose. While on Earth in the physical body, it is given an opportunity to accelerate its own learning process and to achieve a higher consciousness level.

What then is the vehicle through which the soul-consciousness operates?

This may be explained in terms of the subtle bodies. Our human body may be better understood if viewed as an *interface* between the self and the environment around us. All of us are aware of the dense physical environment we are in. However, in addition to this, we have several other less familiar environments that we are unaware of. This includes:

(1) vital energy (etheric environment),
(2) feelings (astral environment),

(3) thoughts (mental environment), and
(4) intuition (causal environment).

As individuals we interface with each of these environments through the different human "bodies".

These different bodies are best described according to the various "planes" of human existence. As seen from the table, our solar system has seven interpenetrating planes of energy fields or planes. Three of these planes, the Physical, the Emotional and the Mental, are directly involved with the human's existence.

PLANE		BODY CONSTITUTION	
DIVINE			
MONADIC		Monad	
ATMIC		Atma	Higher (Spiritual) Self
BUDDHIC		Buddhi	
MENTAL	Higher	Causal Body (Manas)	The Soul
	Lower	Mental Body	
EMOTIONAL		Astral Body	The Psyche
PHYSICAL	Etheric	Etheric Double	
	Dense	Physical Body	

Physical Plane – The physical plane has two parts, the visible and the invisible. The visible (dense) part of the physical body is composed of solids, liquids and gases and is described in great detail in our medical textbooks of anatomy and physiology. The invisible part of the physical body that is not mentioned in our textbooks is called the "etheric double".[11] It is so called because it is a close replica of the dense physical body. This body is made up of finer grades of physical matter that are etheric and atomic.[12]

The etheric double has two functions. Firstly, it absorbs vital energy and distributes the energy to the whole body. Secondly, it acts as a bridge between the brain of the dense physical body and the consciousness of the astral and mental bodies. In health, the etheric double is firmly attached to the dense, physical body. However, in times of accident, shock, death or when under the influence of drugs, anesthesia or hypnosis, the etheric double is separable from the dense body.

Emotional Plane – The emotional (or astral) body is the vehicle of feeling, emotion and desire, and it embraces all the passions of the individual. Since it is composed of astral matter, which is much finer than physical matter, it interpenetrates the physical body. Thus we can conceptualize an astral being who might be occupying the same space as a physical being in the physical world. However, each being could remain unconscious of the other and they would not impede each other's free movement. This principle of interpenetration makes it clear that different realms of nature are not separated in space. Rather they coexist in and around us and are present in the here and now.

The astral body has three functions. Firstly it makes feeling possible and is the storehouse for our desires and emotions. Desire is the essence that manifests in the astral body and is conditioned by it. In its rudimentary form, it is a sensation, but in its complex form it is an emotion. Secondly, the astral body acts as a bridge and a transmitter of vibrations between the mind and physical matter. Thirdly, it acts as an independent vehicle of

---

[11] The etheric double is the name given to a subtle body propounded by theosophy as the lowest layer in the human energy field or aura. It is in immediate contact with the physical body.

[12] Physical matter is made up of seven grades of density: solid, liquid, gaseous, etheric, super-etheric, subatomic and atomic according to occultists in "The Etheric Double" by A.E. Powell, 1925.

consciousness and action. During sleep or trance it is possible for the astral body to separate itself from the physical body and function freely on its own plane. This is commonly known as "astral travel".

Mental Plane – The mental plane also has two main subdivisions: (1) the lower mental plane which contains the "mental body"; and (2) the higher mental plane which contains the "causal body".

The mental body is the vehicle through which the self expresses itself as concrete intellect. In this body, the powers of the lower mind, including memory and imagination, are developed. Its manifestations are usually known as "the mind" in ordinary waking consciousness. It deals with logic, ideas and concrete thoughts.

The causal body exists in the higher mental plane. Its predominant element is that of knowledge and wisdom. It deals with principles, ideals and abstract thoughts and is the repository of our innate knowledge and capabilities. It owes its name to the fact that residing in it are the "causes" which manifest themselves as effects in the outer, visible world. In the causal body also lies the creative power of meditation, and the energies that grow out of one-pointed concentration.

The centrality of the role of the causal body is in reincarnation. One may perceive the causal body as that part of ourselves that reincarnates into lower bodies from one life to another. It is the experience of past lives that is stored in the causal body and that accounts for the general attitude and actions we take towards life.

The causal body continues life after life. In contrast, the mental, emotional and physical bodies are temporary vehicles of one lifetime only and renewed in each incarnation.

The Soul
The soul is considered the link between the individual's divine spirit and his lower personality. It is perceived as being powered by the mind, which works within the limitations of the physical brain. It is also conceptualized as interfacing with its environment

in three ways, corresponding to the physical, astral and mental planes.

With the physical environment, the soul relates to things that present themselves to our physical senses from the external world and we accept them as a given fact. With the astral environment, it turns the world into something that has significance for us and helps us to build up our own inner world of sensations and feelings. However, we do not wander aimlessly from one sense impression to another. So, with the third, mental interface, the soul helps us to think about our sensations and actions, create a rational coherence and establish a goal that we strive for, unceasingly. At the same time, it makes the moral goodness in ourselves come alive and make us a member of the higher spiritual order.

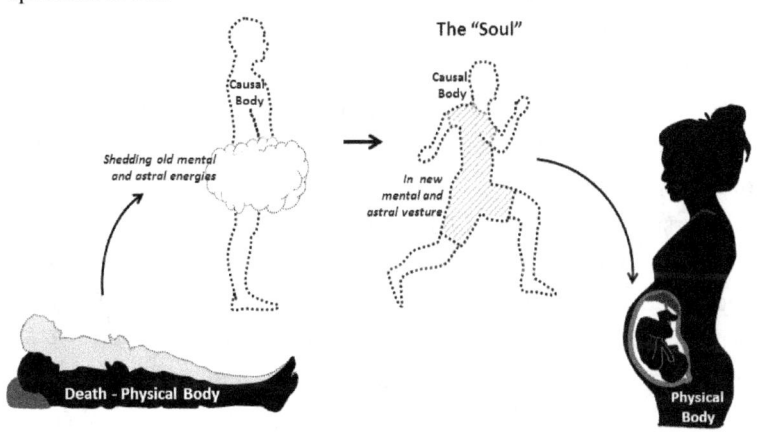

As the soul makes its continuing journey from one incarnation to another, it repeatedly passes through the three "worlds" of the physical, emotional and mental planes. When a soul finishes his stay in the formless world of the higher mental plane in one lifetime, he begins his new life-period by putting forth his energies of the form-world in the lower mental plane. Next, the causal body becomes clothed with his new mental and astral vestures that express the faculties inherited from his previous lives. Finally, he is drawn by forces to the womb which provides him with a suitable physical body. This marks the beginning of a new cycle of rebirth.

Before an individual is born, his soul selects a series of goals and life lessons for his time on Earth. This is a form of sacred contract that he makes with the Divine and determines what kind of a life he is going to live. The soul is therefore on a never-ending journey of learning and evolution through reincarnation.

The Earth may therefore be looked upon as a "schoolhouse" for the soul who has chosen to come down to the physical plane to learn. The current lifetime is his opportunity to encounter what he needs in order to grow on a soul level. One way to understand this evolutionary process is to compare our entire lifespan in our current lifetime on Earth as being equivalent to a single day in the life of our soul in this evolutionary journey.

Each of our souls has created a basic Life Plan prior to our current incarnation. This includes the form our life purpose will take. While we choose our experiences before coming to Earth, we do not plan our entire lives. That would be boring! Rather we only devise the major intersections and overall themes that form our personal lessons from which we will learn.

For the patient undergoing regression therapy, helping him to become aware of the lessons that he has learned – or failed to learn – in previous lifetimes enables him to understand how these can lead to unexplained emotional problems in his current life.

The physical brain of a man cannot normally remember his past lives because it neither has a memory nor a record of a past incarnation in which it did not participate. Likewise, the astral and mental bodies are all new for each incarnation. The causal body is the only body that persists from one lifetime to another. Given the imperfect state of communication between the soul and the lower human personality, recall of past life experiences is difficult if not impossible for most people.

Further Reading

Bennet, G., *The Wound and the Doctor: Healing, Technology and Power in Modern Medicine*, **Secker & Warburg, 1987** – This interesting book is written by a doctor who started his career as a surgeon and went on to become a psychotherapist and psychiatrist. He addresses the issue of why many doctors are unhappy with the work they do and many patients are unhappy about the care they receive, and how things could be better. He also dwells on the role of complementary therapies.

Churchill, R., *Regression Hypnotherapy – Transcripts of Transformation*, **Transforming Press, 2002** – This book contains teaching material and full transcripts of current life regression sessions for a variety of conditions including phobias, grief, lack of confidence, sabotaging success, unhealthy relationships, abuse and fear of abandonment. It is an excellent guide for beginners, as well as a useful reference for experienced therapists.

LaBay, M.L., *Past Life Regression: A Guide for Practitioners*, **Trafford Publishing, 2004** – A light reading book on the practice of past life therapy that incorporates stories from the author's personal experience. The author blends hypnotherapy techniques with philosophy, intuition and reincarnation theory to catalyze growth and transformation in her clients.

Lucas, W.B., *Regression Therapy: A Handbook for Professionals, Vols I & II*, **Book Solid Press, 1992** – The two volumes are a classic for regression therapists. It is a multi-author work on regression therapy compiled by a professional psychologist and Jungian analyst. Volume I focuses on past life therapy while Volume II touches on prenatal and birth experiences, childhood traumas and death.

Moody, H.R., *The Five Stages of the Soul – Charting the Spiritual Passages that Shape our Lives,* **Anchor Books, 1997** – An inspiring book in which the author interweaves psychology with spirituality and maps out a path of how people search for meaning and self-discovery and moves from the secular to the sacred.

Pollack, R., *Seventy Eight Degrees of Wisdom,* **Thorson, 1997** – A definitive text on the Tarot, written by a renowned authority on the subject, for those who want to pursue the standard meanings of the Tarot in some detail.

TenDam, H., *Deep Healing,* **Tasso, 1996** – This is a comprehensive textbook of regression therapy techniques used by Hans TenDam, who is one of the pioneers in regression therapy. The book can be ordered from Hans' email: tasso@damconsult.nl.

Tomlinson, A., *Healing the Eternal Soul,* **From the Heart Press, 2012** – This is a definitive reference work in regression therapy. The author shares his valuable experience in detail and uses concrete case studies to illustrate his points and techniques. It is a captivating book and a must-have for all students of regression therapy.

Tomlinson, A. (ed.), *Transforming the Eternal Soul,* **From the Heart Press, 2011** – This book is packed with illuminating case studies and specialized therapy techniques. The chapters include: empowering a client; working with difficult clients; spiritual inner child regression; clearing dark energy; crystal therapy in regression; spiritual emergency; and integrating therapy into a client's current life.

Woolger, R.J., *Healing Your Past Lives,* **Sounds True Inc., 2004** – This short book provides a series of interesting case studies that illustrate the power of uncovering past lives in the healing process. It gives insight as to how current life symptoms could be related to past life dramas and frozen memories. It also provides the reader with the key to unlocking the mysteries and questions they struggle with in their current lives.

Woolger, R.J., ***Other Lives, Other Selves – A Jungian Psychotherapist Discovers Past Lives,*** **Bantam Books, 1988** – This is a fascinating book that presents the author's original insights into the emerging psychology of reincarnation. The book draws on both Western science and Eastern spirituality and explains how past lives may form the basis of transformation and healing in our lives.

Regression Therapy Associations

Society for Medical Advance and Research in Regression Therapy (SMAR-RT)
This international society, formed in April 2013, aims to conduct and coordinate research in regression therapy. It is led by medical doctors who share the vision to bring about the integration of complementary and holistic approaches into conventional Medicine. It is a non-profit organization and hopes to raise awareness of the effectiveness of regression therapy as a healing tool within the medical profession.
Website: http://www.smar-rt.com

Earth Association of Regression Therapy (EARTh)
This is an independent association with the objective to create and maintain an international standard in regression therapy and improve and enlarge its professional acceptance. Every summer it offers a series of workshops for ongoing professional development. It aims to advance the field by providing a meeting ground for regression therapists through conferences and meetings.
Website: http://www.earth-association.org

Spiritual Regression Therapy Association (SRTA)
This is an international association of regression therapists that respect the spiritual nature of their clients. Established by Andy Tomlinson, they are professionally trained by the *Past Life Regression Academy* to international standards and work to a code of ethics that respects the clients' welfare.
Website: http://www.regressionassociation.com

Association for Regression and Reincarnation Research (ARRR)
This association was founded by Dr. Newton Kondaveti and launched in Hyderabad, India, in 2010 with the aim to promote research in regression and reincarnation, and work towards increasing awareness and acceptance of past life therapy among people in India and all over the world. It publishes a newsletter, a magazine, holds annual conventions and conducts certification examinations for professionals practicing past life regression therapy.
Website: http://www.arrrglobal.org

International Board of Regression Therapy (IBRT)
This is an independent examining and certifying board for past life therapists, researchers and training programs. Its mission is to set professional standards for regression therapists and organizations. The website has a list of international accredited past life and regression therapy training organizations.
Website: http://www.ibrt.org

The Authors

Dr. Nicole Lee obtained her medical degree from the Yong Loo School of Medicine, National University of Singapore. Her interest in Finance has led her to complete a Master degree in Finance. She currently practices as a general medical practitioner while pursuing her interests in writing and trading.
Contact: nicole.leesq@gmail.com

Dr. Peter Mack is a medical graduate from the University of Singapore and specializes in General Surgery, holding Fellowships from the Royal College of Surgeons of Edinburgh, and the Royal College of Physicians and Surgeons of Glasgow. He obtained his PhD in Medical Science from Lund University, Sweden; MBA from the Business School of the National University of Singapore; Master in Health Economics from Curtin University; and Master in Medical Education from the University of Dundee. He is a certified hypnotherapist with NGH, IMDHA, a graduate of the Past Life Regression Academy and a founding member of the Society for Medical Advance and Research with Regression Therapy (SMAR-RT). He is the author of the books *Healing Deep Hurt Within*, and *Life-Changing Moments in Inner Healing*.
Contact: dr.pmack@gmail.com

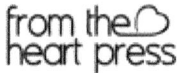

Healing Deep Hurt Within

(Swedish and French editions also available)

Author: Dr. Peter Mack

This book is based on a true story of an emotionally traumatized lady who suffered from unexplained syncope, dissociative amnesia, insomnia, auditory hallucinations and suicidal tendencies. She recovered from her devastated state after intensive regression therapy over an 18-day period. She underwent transformational healing and moved on in life. Upon recovery, she requested that her physician-therapist write up the story of her healing journey.

"A book that touches my heart." – Rudy Phen, Physician

"I couldn't put the book down, and finished reading it in three hours. It has been almost a week, and I can still feel the effect." – Swan Ang, Management Trainer

"The drama is overwhelming. There is a sense of liberation after reading it." – Leong Saw Wei, Managing Director

"This book is a must-read for those who are ready to assume responsibility and live their life to the fullest." – Theresa Chee, Life Coach

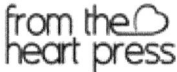

Life-Changing Moments in Inner Healing

Author: Dr. Peter Mack

This book contains the regression stories of four patients who went through past life healing. The first patient experienced unexplained visions of an unidentified lady and water phobia and resolved his issues through past life regression. The second patient was faced with serious problems of procrastination and anger management since childhood. The third patient had problems of memory loss, and fear of success and public speaking. The fourth patient was afflicted with an irrational fear of snakes. All four patients went through transformational healing after regression therapy.

"I read this amazing book in one sitting and just couldn't put it down." – Rosa Lilia Castillo Maya, Housewife

"A highly recommended book for those seeking alternative healing therapies." – Joyce Cheng, Neurofeedback Therapist

"This book joins a deserving place alongside Dr. Weiss' book on my bookshelf." – Tan Cheen Chong, Technology Marketing Specialist

from the heart press

Inner Healing Journey – A Medical Perspective

Edited by: Dr. Peter Mack
Contributing Authors:
Dr. Peter Mack, Dr. Soumya Rao, Dr. Karin Maier-Henle, Dr. Sergio Werner Bauer, Dr. Moacir Oliveira, Dr. Natwar Sharma

This book contains the stories of eleven patients who went through regression therapy for various issues and problems including marriage crisis, inner child healing, self-love and self-destructive issues, struggling to love, refractory asthma, chronic pain of fibromyalgia, systemic lupus erythematosus and infertility.

> *"The stories are incredibly inspiring and healing with a powerful impact. I highly recommend this book to those who want to make positive changes in themselves."*
> – Shirley Tay, Holistic Therapist

> *"This is a remarkable book on the marvels of regression therapy. It is a must-read for all healthcare professionals and therapists in holistic healing,"*
> – Wendy Yeung, Holistic Therapist

www.ingramcontent.com/pod-product-compliance
Lightning Source LLC
Chambersburg PA
CBHW051943290426
44110CB00015B/2091